ART DECO TRAVELLER
A Guide to the USA

To Elizabeth, Elijah, Theodore, & Eliana
My American Family

ART DECO TRAVELLER

A Guide to the USA

Edited by E. Riggs

Art Deco Publisher, 2020

Printed by Melita Press

Art Deco Publisher
Kemp House, 152 City Road, LONDON EC1V 2NX
artdeco-traveller.co.uk

Art Deco Traveller ®
Text Genista Davidson ©
This edition Art Deco Publisher ©

ISBN 978-0-9934146-1-9
The moral right of the author has been asserted

Art Deco Traveller ®

CONTENTS

INTRODUCTION

Defining Art Deco is not always easy, over the years and to this day debates have ensued; however, one certainty is that many facets are involved with this unique architectural, style and design.

As Art Deco crossed all genres and all boundaries, we see a profusion of interpretations. These buildings often incorporate the national identities of the Country or State, displayed in the bas-reliefs or patterned materials that adorn the facades. You can find the bold domineering skyscrapers in New York to the tropical Deco in Florida. We shall take a journey across to the West Coast and discover the legacy that deco left in cities such as Los Angeles and Hollywood.

This book does not profess in any way to include all hotels, monuments or places of interest in the Art Deco style in the USA, due partly to page constraints. However, it has a clear overview of the notable worthy contenders in various States. Some areas may not be able to boast of many hotels in the Art Deco design; however, they do have other notable buildings from when this style of architecture was at its height.

Poetic licence has also prevailed, as some of the hotels may not be architecturally Art Deco, however, being from the period they possess the glamour and nostalgia associated so clearly with the Jazz Age. I hope this guide will whet your appetite to further investigate the vast and diverse Art Deco architecture and design that is on offer for all to see in this magnificent Country. Your first port of call should always involve seeking out the specific Art Deco Societies, and many States have these. They are a brilliant source of information and collectively celebrate and champion the heritage and legacy of Art Deco in their region.

Enjoy your Art Deco travels!

ALABAMA

Capital: Montgomery
Became the 22nd State: 1819
Flower: Camellia
Bird: Yellowhammer

ACCOMMODATION

Admiral Hotel
251 Government Street, Mobile, AL 36602

Originally opened in 1940 and was the first hotel in Mobile to have the extravagance of a telephone in every room and the luxury of air-conditioning. Many celebrities have walked through its doors including Elvis Presley, James Stewart, and Bob Hope.

In 2014 it was sold and the new owners totally redesigned it with the opulent Art Deco style lobby and updated the entire 150 guestrooms. The exterior with its minimal architecture belies the interior, with its original Art Deco elevator doors, chandelier and marble floors. It has 5 luxurious suites on the top floor and is part of the Historic Hotels of America.

Hotel Indigo Birmingham Five Points
1023 20th Street South, Birmingham AL 35205

This eight-storey building was originally commissioned as a Medical Arts building exclusively for Doctors and Surgeons of the area and opened in 1931.

A local architect *Charles H. McCauley* utilised the lower floor as retail shops and the Apothecary. After changing hands and uses several times over the years, it was first opened as a hotel in 1988 by a retired Surgeon. It consists of 63 guest rooms and suites and is located near to the buzzing epicentre of clubs, restaurants and bars.

The Redmont Hotel
2101 Fifth Avenue North, Birmingham AL 35203

The Redmont is housed in an impressive fourteen storey 1925 building. It was totally renovated and

refurbished in 2016 and has fortunately not lost its original features. These consist of marble staircase and iron hand rail, along with

the high vaulted ceilings with decorative mouldings which complement the ten-foot crystal chandelier. It has 120 guest rooms and suites. These are all in a clean fresh, contemporary modern style. It has a café, restaurant and particularly nice rooftop cocktail bar. This historic hotel is part of the Curio collection by Hilton, and is within easy walking distance to the theatre district.

Battle House Renaissance Hotel & Spa
Downtown, Mobile AL 36602

A hotel has stood on this site since 1852, albeit that the original burnt down and the current Battle House was designed by *Frank Andrews* of New York in 1908. It has a colourful past and has been host to President Woodrow Wilson in 1913 and many eminent people over the years.

In 1974 due to the economic downturn especially in this area of the town, it sadly closed and lay abandoned until 2001 when a regeneration programme brought it back to life.

It is now a four-diamond star hotel with 238 guest rooms including 31 suites and once again draws in the celebrities and guests wanting to experience the glamour and style of a historic age. The hotels, restaurants, spa and crystal ballroom, all live up to the grandeur of a lost age.

The combination of styles, Edwardian, Art Deco and Contemporary all merge well creating a luxurious and glamourous hotel with a by-gone ambience.

OUT & ABOUT

The Princess Theatre
112 2ⁿᵈ Avenue NE, Decatur AL 35601

In 1919 this former livery stable was transformed into a thriving vaudeville playhouse and silent film venue. Not until 1941 did the Princess emerge with its Art Deco façade and interior design opening with the film 'Tom, Dick and Harry' staring Ginger Rogers.

Fortunately, the Art Deco still remains, with its large neon sign, unmistakable central fin and curvilinear box office with glass bricks, it certainly ticks all the right boxes! Local architect *Albert Frahn* decorated the auditorium in burgundy and grey walls with murals that glow in a black lighting system.

The Ritz Theatre
115 Court Square North, Talladega AL 35160

Originally constructed circa 1936 this theatre is considered to be one of the best surviving examples of Art Deco main street theatres of the 1930s.

The lavish façade comprises exclusively of structured glass.

The foyer is a marvel in shades of green trimmed in black and chromium. The auditorium walls are colourful incorporating red, green, gold, black and chromium cornices. The theatre has been meticulously restored, sourcing original materials from the period and reopened its doors in 1998.

Alabama Theatre
1817 3rd Ave North, Birmingham AL 35203

The Alabama Theatre was built in 1927 by Paramount Studios to showcase their films. It has been fully utilised for film, concerts, vaudeville and even the Mickey Mouse Club.

After its total renovation in the late 1990s, it has been returned back to its former glory and you cannot visit Alabama with experiencing a night out here. The unmissable large neon sign outside entices theatre goers to feast their eyes on the gold ceilings, embellishments and adornments. With 2,500 seats to choose from, each with mesmerising views of the interior and a spectacular Wurlitzer, it's no wonder this is a designated official state historic theatre.

Opposite the Alabama Theatre is the Lyric, which is also an absolute jewel of a venue, although not in the Art Deco style it is well worth a visit.

The interior
of the Lyric
Theatre.

Alabama Power Company Building
600 North 18th Street, AL 35203

This impressive 1925 commercial building is dominated by elongated piers juxtaposed with recessed windows and black glass. Above the entrance are three sculptured figures representing Power, Heat and Light.

Decorative bands of marble and coloured brick appear above the piers which make up patterns of crosses and circles. It has a pitched hipped roof with the crowning glory of the figure Electra in bronze with gold leaf. These worthy sculptured figures are the work of John Field Stanford Junior, a New York sculptor.

Birmingham City Hall & Library
710 20th Street AL 35203

The Architect *Charles McCauley*, designed this impressive ten-storey building, in 1950. It consists of a taller central section with recessed side wings.

It is coated in limestone and granite with the deeply recessed panels staggered either side. It's a fine example of 1950s Moderne architecture, proving that this style was still in vogue.

John Carroll High School
300 Lakeshore Parkway, Birmingham AL 35209

Construction for this High School began in 1946 in the Modernist architectural style not unlike the Bauhaus style from the 1920s, functional with clean clear lines.

ALASKA

Capital: Juneau
Became the 49th State: 1959
Mineral: Gold
Official Sport: Dog Mushing

ACCOMMODATION

Westmark Baranof Hotel
127 North Franklin Street, Juneau,
Alaska 99801
1939

This hotel has 215 guestrooms and suites over nine floors. It has a fine restaurant and a cocktail bar called the Bubble Room, or the less formal cafe and lounge.

The Art Deco entrance marquee and streamline exterior, are further complemented with the original artwork, by Alaskan artists *Eustace Ziegler* and *Sydney Laurence* displayed in the public areas. It is conveniently centrally located in downtown and a short distance from the cruise ship dock.

Historic Anchorage Hotel
330 E Street, Anchorage, Alaska AK 99501
1936

This hotel has an illustrious past with its share of fall and decline. It was not until 1989 that its 26 guest rooms were brought back to life. It has been frequented by artists and dignitaries and even has a resident ghost! The exterior of the building is Art Deco in design and the interior is contemporary modern.

OUT & ABOUT

Alaska State Capitol
120 4th St, Juneau, Alaska, AK99801
1931

This six-story building is constructed of brick faced reinforced concrete, the facade being of Indiana limestone on the first two floors. The four columns which stand in the portico are made of Tokeen marble from the Prince of Wales Island. The lobby has clay murals 'Harvest of the Land' and 'Harvest of the Sea'. A bust of the Alaska Native activist *Elizabeth Peratrovich* is proudly displayed in the lobby. The executive office doors are

made of black birch, with hand carvings depicting Alaskan industry.

Fourth Avenue Theatre
630 W 4th Avenue, Anchorage, Alaska AK 99501
1941-47 B. Marcus Priteca & Augustine A. Porreca

This historical landmark operated as a cinema until the 1980s and it is often considered the best example of Art Deco in Alaska. It is championed by the 'Friends of the Fourth Avenue Theatre' who rightfully want to see it preserved and thrive for future generations. It is currently undergoing restoration phases.

Fairbanks Ice Museum
500 Second Avenue, Fairbanks Alaska, AK 99701
1939 B. Marcus Priteca

This remarkable Art Deco building was originally the Lacey Street Theatre and is listed on the National Register of Historic Places. It closed its doors in 1981 and it was not until 1992 that it was fully renovated, restored and repurposed.

It reopened as the Museum of Ice Sculpture, and has comprehensive demonstrations and presentations throughout the year.

Fairbanks City Hall
800 Cushman St, Fairbanks, Alaska. AK 99701
1934-1935 Tourtellotte & Hummel

Fairbanks has a fine City Hall, well worth a visit. It is set back from the road and its central column is in symmetrical harmony with its wings either side.

Old Federal Building
Cushman St and 3rd Ave, Fairbanks, Alaska, AK 99501
1933 George N. Ray

When this building was constructed it was the most northern example of a concrete construction in the U.S. It is a 3-story building and it has the exterior feature of v-shaped grooves within the pilasters that separate the columns of the windows.

Aluminium panels enhance the detail and the concrete grooves are abundant on the spandrels on the upper building. It is well worth a visit inside this Alaskan Police Station, if only to see the terrazzo flooring and marble floors and walls. Step a little further into the courtroom to marvel at the copper ceiling.

Cape Decision Lighthouse
Kuiu Island, Southeast Alaska
1932 U.S. Lighthouse Service

This Modernist building has a square tower 23 metres high and made of concrete. The purpose of the building obviously lends itself well to the design, as the bulk mass can withstand the elements.

Cape Hinchinbrook Lighthouse
Southern end of Hinchinbrook Island, Alaska
1910 first lit in 1934

This reinforced concrete tower with Art Deco features is 20 metres high and has a white tower with black lantern. The tower has a distinct design, incorporating recesses and curvilinear features.

Cape Spencer Lighthouse
Glacier Bay National Park and Preserve, Alaska
1925

This lighthouse with a short tower and black painted balcony are distinctively in the Art Deco style. It is 32 metres focal height.

© *lighthousefriends.com*

ARIZONA

Capital: Phoenix
Became the 48th State: 1912
Gem: Turquoise
Bird: Cactus Wren

ACCOMMODATION

Arizona Biltmore Hotel
2400 East Missouri Avenue, Phoenix AZ 85016
1929 Albert Chase McArthur

This hotel will always have the kudos of *Frank Lloyd Wright's* stamp on it, owing to his influence and input. For a short time, *Wright* was a consulting architect on the project and *Albert Chase McArthur*, had studied under *Wright*, when he was a Harvard graduate.

The hotel which is part of the Waldorf Astoria group, is unique in its construction, as it is made up of 250,000 blocks, made from the desert sand. Named Biltmore blocks, they were cut in 34 different geometric patterns. The hotel soon became known as the 'Jewel of the Desert'.

It has 740 guest rooms and suites, but surprisingly never feels over busy, due to the spacious design and the fact that it is set in 39 acres. It has beautiful gardens and grounds including the World class golf course, all set at the foot of the Phoenix Mountains. This legendary hotel has hosted Presidents, film stars and musicians over the years. Irving Berlin wrote 'I'm Dreaming of a White Christmas' here whilst soaking up the sun, and Clark Gable and Carole Lombard honeymooned here.

Hilton Garden Inn Downtown

15 East Monroe Street, Phoenix AZ 85004
1932 Morgan, Walls & Clements

This impressive Art Deco skyscraper was initially built for the Valley Bank of Arizona. It then transformed into the Hotel Monroe, before standing empty for 30 years until 2015, when it reopened in all its glory.

It has original Art Deco features in the grand lobby with a 24ft high ceiling, lined with deco columns and marble floors. The original doors and brass fittings are also still in situ.

It is also famous for being featured in Hitchcock's opening scenes to the film 'Psycho' in 1960. It has 170 guest rooms and suites, all in a modern contemporary style. Also, Monroe's lobby bar, pays homage to its history.

Apache Lodge Motel

1130 East Gurley Street, Prescott AZ 86301
1946

The exterior of this stepped facade motel, has little changed since it was built. Originally the inner

courtyard had a swimming pool and bar when it was operated as a hotel, however, these have long gone. It offers two types of room, deluxe and economy at very reasonable rates.

Grand Highland Hotel
154 S. Montezuma, Prescott AZ 86303

A hotel has stood on this site since 1903. Unfortunately, due to a fire in 2012 the original hotel was badly damaged and this family ran business was redeveloped with a new approach.

It has twelve historically themed rooms and the Speak Easy guest room is designed to incorporate the flavour of the Art Deco jazz period with the colour scheme and furnishings.

It offers a continental breakfast and afternoon refreshments with nearby restaurants.

OUT & ABOUT

Old Phoenix City Hall / Maricopa County Courthouse
125 W. Washington Street, Phoenix AZ 85003
1928 Lescher & Mahoney, Edward Neild

This building is a fusion of Art Deco, Spanish Colonial Revival and Renaissance Revival styles.

From 1928 to 1994 it was Phoenix City Hall; the current use is the Maricopa County Courthouse and Phoenix Police Museum.

Inside it has retained many original features with the ceilings, light fixtures, staircases and old mail chutes.

Former Hotel Westward Ho/Senior Housing complex
618 North Central Avenue, Phoenix AZ
1927 Fisher, Lake and Traver

This building was a luxury hotel from 1928 to 1979, and in 1981 it was converted to a senior housing complex. Over the years it has seen it fair share of famous people including Richard Nixon, Ronald Reagan (who was an actor at that time), and John F. Kennedy who visited the restaurant in 1961, that was on the 15th floor. In 1949 the antenna was added which is actually 60 foot taller than the building itself. It is an impressive building to view from the exterior.

Luhrs City Center

These two buildings in downtown Phoenix were designed and sponsored by George Luhrs originally from Germany. He was a successful real estate developer from 1881 to 1929. It was the El Paso architectural firm who were responsible for both buildings and Trost & Trost the architects came up with two related but quite different buildings. The Luhrs Building of 1924 and the Lhurs Tower of 1929.

Lhurs Tower
11 W. Jefferson Street, #100 Phoenix AZ 85003
1929 Trost & Trost

This 13-storey building is still utilised for office space, as it was originally intended. It has copper ornamentation and intricate carved details adorning the exterior. The front lobby is wonderfully preserved, as is the elevator.

Phoenix Title and Trust/Orpheum Lofts
114 West Adams Street, Phoenix AZ 85003
1931 Leschder & Mahoney

From 1931 to 2003 this was the Phoenix Title and Trust office building and was championed for its modernist style.

In 2003 when it was transformed into 90 residential lofts, much of the original interior was lost. However, the marble floors, metal doors and travertine are gloriously in situ in the main lobby.

Residential Apartments formerly the Hotel San Carlos Hotel
106 East 1st Street, Yuma AZ 85364
c.1930

The once famous San Carlos Hotel has seen many stars and their crew in its heyday, as it used to be a regular for the visiting film entourages.

It fell into disrepair and was redesigned as residential apartments for the retired in 1997. It is listed on the National Register of Historic Places, therefore has retained its original exterior features of neon sign and opal glass letters. The inside lobby is also beautifully preserved.

Cochise County Courthouse
100 Quality Hill Road, Bisbee AZ 85603
1931 Roy W. Place

This purpose-built court house is absolutely magnificent and well worth visiting. The ornate exterior decoration is complimented by the stunning brass doors.

Phelps Dodge Mercantile Company
Bisbee AZ 85603
1939 Del Webb

Originally a department store. Phelps-Dodge was a dominant force in Bisbee history, as the company owned the mines, hospital and practically the whole town, including the newspaper.

ARKANSAS

Capital: Little Rock
Became the 25th State: 1836
Flower: Apple Blossom
Gem: Diamond

PUBLIC LIBRARY, PINE BLUFF, ARK.—13

ACCOMMODATION

The Waters
340 Central Ave, Hot Springs, AR 71901
1913 George R. Mann

This historic building in the neoclassical style has been renovated and restored to a boutique hotel with 62 guest rooms. It is situated in the natural beauty spot of Hot Springs National Park on Bathhouse Row.

The guest rooms are modern contemporary in design and the Avenue restaurant offers southern artisan style cuisine. The Space bar and relaxing spa facilities complement this small private hotel.

Arlington Resort Hotel & Spa
239 Central Ave, Hot Springs National Park, AR 71901
1924 Mann & Stern

This Landmark hotel has a rich history of famous and infamous guests. Al Capone rented the entire fourth floor and it was a haven to other gangsters during the 1930s.

Suite 443 was his favourite and is called the Al Capone Suite should you wish to stay in his room.

It has two restaurants, a spa and two outdoor pools and thermal baths.

Hotel Seville
302 N Main St, Harrison, AR 72601

This hotel originally opened in 1929 and after several changes in ownership over the decades, it was in 2008 that this historic building underwent an extensive restoration programme and reopened in 2012.

The architectural style is Spanish Revival, incorporating resplendent Arabic inscriptions and wall decorations. It houses *Cafe 1929* which has furnishings relating to the era, adding to the overall ambience of this atmospheric hotel.

OUT & ABOUT

Bathhouse Row

This is a collection of bathhouses and associated buildings and gardens that are located at Hot Springs National Park in the city of Hot Springs Arkansas. They are situated on Central Avenue between Reserve and Fountain Streets. The championed architect *Walter T. Bailey* (1881-1941) was responsible for Union Bath House and the First Church of Deliverance in Chicago, Illinois.

Bathhouse Row consists of eight bathhouse buildings that were constructed between the years of 1892 and 1923 along the Grand Promenade in parklands. This interesting piece of social history and architecture was designated a National Historic Landmark district in 1987.

Bathhouses are as follows: -
The Lamar Bathhouse opened in 1923 replacing a Victorian structure. It has a Spanish flavour of design. It now houses the park's office management and archives.

© *NPS*

33

The Buckstaff Bathhouse designed by *Frank W. Gibb* architects has been in continual operation since opening in 1912 following a rebuild after the original bathhouse was destroyed by fire. The ornate interior is very reminiscent of the Golden Age of Bathing. It has a current capacity of 1,000 bathers per day.

© NPS

© NPS

Ozark Bathhouse was designed by *Mann and Stern* of Little Rock and opened in 1922. It closed in 1977 as a bathhouse and is now houses the Hot Springs National Park Cultural Centre.

The Quapaw Bathhouse is the longest building on the row and opened in 1922. The mosaic tiled dome is most impressive. It closed in 1984 and was repurposed as a family spa in 2008.

© NPS

The Fordyce designed by *Mann and Stern* opened in 1915. It is the largest bathhouse on the row and the first to go out of business in 1962. Today it is historically furnished museum and serves as the park's visitor centre.

© NPS

The impressive Maurice Bathhouse opened in 1912 and was designed by *George Gleim*. During the 1930s a therapeutic pool was situated in the basement and it was the only bathhouse on the row to have a pool. It closed in 1974. The Hale Bathhouse consists of the oldest structures on the row dated to 1892. It was remodelled in the classical revival style in 1914, it is now closed.

The last Bathhouse aptly named the Superior, now contains the only brewery in a United States National Park. It utilizes the thermal spring water to make their beer. It opened in 1916 and was designed by *Harry Schwebke* with a classical revival origin.

Arkansas County Courthouse
Southern District, 101 Court Square 6, De Witt, AR 72042
1931 H. Ray Burks

This courthouse is typical in the design of many in the US, as it is symmetrical with set-backs and displays a stepped façade.

Arkansas Louisiana Gas Company Building
116 West 6th Avenue, Pine Bluff, AR 71601
1950 Mitchell Selligman

This single storey building is of significant interest in design and is listed on the NRHP. The parapet has blue flame-shaped finials at the ends of the central raised section. The walls include blocks of clear and coloured glass with tile elements.

Arkansas Tuberculosis Sanatorium
256 Carey Rd,Booneville, AR 72927
1909 Haralson & Mott, Erhart & Eichenbaum

This large campus covers 800 acres and was the main hospital for the treatment of TB, up until 1973 when it closed. The campus is now owned by the state and patients of the Booneville Development Centre are housed in some of the buildings. In 2006 it was added to the NRHP.

Florida Brothers Building
319 W. Hale St, Osceola, AR 72370
1936 Thomas P. Florida

This seemingly insignificant little building was listed on the NRHP in 1987. It is a single storey structure built of cut stone with a flat roof. Being a commercial outlet, this refined Art Deco style is a fine example of the effort that was made, to beautify what could have been a mundane building.

Courtesy of the Arkansas
Historic Preservation Program

Fort Smith Masonic Temple
200 North 11th St, Fort Smith, AR 72901
1929 George R. Mann

This four-storey building constructed in Bedford stone in the Egyptian Revival style has three large banquet halls, and auditorium seating for 1,200 people. It is utilised for meetings, special events and stage productions.

Hempstead County Courthouse
NW Corner of 5th and Washington St, Hope, AR 71801
1939 B.W. Edwards

Throughout the state of Arkansas many courthouses are built in the modernist style as a boom in public service buildings spread throughout the country with the WPA. The modernist style incorporated many elements of the neoclassical revival and symmetrical stepped cubic design.

CALIFORNIA

Capital: Sacramento
Became the 31st State: 1850
Tree: Redwood
Rock: Serpentine

ACCOMMODATION

Sunset Tower Hotel
8358 Sunset Boulevard, Los Angeles CA 90069
1929-31 Leland A. Bryant

Originally this building was the upmarket
Sunset Tower apartment block until being
converted into this luxurious hotel. It has
a sultry deco exterior with curvy
contours and stunning views of the strip.

It can boast of once being home to the
likes of Errol Flynn, Elizabeth Taylor,
Frank Sinatra and Marilyn Monroe. The
author of the Great Gatsby, *F. Scott
Fitzgerald* spent his last days in Hollywood
at Sunset Towers. It has 74 guestrooms and suites elegantly designed and
decorated in a modern contemporary style. To complete this it has a poolside
terrace and the Tower bar.

The Cadillac Hotel
8 Dudley Avenue, Venice Beach, California 90291
1914

It was *Abbott Kinney* who set out to create an Italian Venice in California, in 1905. His vision was not shared with the local developers and eventually Venice became known as "Coney Island of the Pacific".

The area known as Venice had become a unique blend of culture, complete with canals and gondola rides, and amusement piers. To help house the boom of travellers, the Cadillac Hotel was built in 1914.

The exterior of the hotel has leanings to Art Deco with its geometric designs and the interior is a fresh contemporary style. Venice beach has seen its changes over the years, but it maintains its unique characteristics. Once a favourite spot of Charlie Chaplin, the city remains a modern-day bohemian destination. Performances such as flame throwers, glass walkers, comedians, and dancers to name a few thrive in this district.

Queen Mary Ship Hotel
1126 Queens Hwy, Long Beach, CA 90802
1936 Construction by John Brown & Co. Clydebank

The Queen Mary Ship started life in 1936 sailing the ocean waves in all her splendour and glory. She had an illustrious life at sea being host to Royalty, screen stars and all the celebrities of her day. It was in 1965 when unfortunately, Cunard

were operating at a loss (due to the increase of air travel) that she retired. Since 1967 she has now been permanently docked at Long beach in California.   It is magnificent to see her in all her original glory; it is a floating temple to 1930s ocean travel.   There are frequent daily tours of the ship, however, I can assure you that if you go for a visit you will most definitely want to stay. This floating hotel has numerous rooms and suites to choose from in varying prices.   However, if you choose the standard rooms, these also have all the original charm of a bygone age, with polished wood panelling and furnishings. The whole package is a nostalgia trip, so definitely pack your period clothing.

Millenium Biltmore Hotel
506 South Grand Avenue, Los Angeles, CA 900071
1923

This hotel can boast that Presidents and the entire 'hoi pollo' over the decades, have chosen it as their favourite haunt. It has also been used for countless movies and backdrop scenes. It just oozes Hollywood glamour everywhere you look.   Crystal chandeliers and opulent lighting showcase the frescos, murals and embroidered tapestries adoring the walls.   You will

certainly feel every bit a million dollars and part of the film set staying here. All the rooms and suites are classically and stylishly decorated, the standard rooms are my favourite as they are decorated with calming warm tones and reasonably priced. The hotels history from the 1920s and 1930s is written in the grand exterior and main public spaces, so prepare to

be dazzled.

Blending contemporary design with Art Deco, DECA is a new residential development bordering San Diego's Hillcrest and North Park neighbourhoods. Acknowledging its

aesthetic debt to Art Deco. DECA announced a cooperative relationship with the estate of Art Deco artist Tamara de Lempicka to exhibit her artwork on site decasandiego.com

---

The Hollywood Roosevelt
7000 Hollywood Blvd, Los Angeles, CA 90028
1927 Fisher, Lake & Traver

This 12-story high building with 300 guest rooms and suites is billed as a modern Hollywood revival and it is certainly aesthetically pleasing from the outside. Designed in the Spanish Colonial style it leans much more to the modernist Art Deco architectural style, it has a gleaming white exterior, with the prominent middle tower, and symmetrically matching wings.

The interior is contemporary modern with a twist of vintage Victorian retro if that is possible. However, it all seems to fit nicely together and the standard rooms are in my taste, the best option in terms of conjuring up the bygone era in furnishing and decor.

Hollywood Historic Hotel
5162 Melrose Ave, Los Angeles, CA 90038
1927 S.Charles Lee

This hotel is not Art Deco on the exterior or interior, however. it does exude that Great Gatsby feel and has lots of added bonuses, including the Art Deco decor of the Edmon Bar.

Due to its close proximity to Paramount film studios it

attracted the film stars of the day. It has, like many hotels, an illustrious past, and had an uncertain future during the forthcoming decades.

It was during the 1970s that it started its second life after its decline and this was due to the storefront renters Edmon's Furniture & Stone gallery who began restoring the hotel back to its former glory. Edmon Simonian, was the fourth generation of highly skilled carpenters. He had great aspirations of one day owning the entire building and reopening the hotel. Due to his hard work and dedication that's exactly what happened. He employed S. Charles Lee, the eminent and prolific theatre designer of the day to bring his project to fruition. What we have today is a luxuriant red brick exterior complete with ornamentation and an interior equally reminiscent of the heady days of the 1920s and 30s.

My top tip here to ask for a room with views of the Hollywood signage which is on level three. You can also get great views of the sign a couple of streets from

the hotel and it is only a short distance from the *walk of fame.*

The Edmon bar is enchanting with splendid Art Deco decor. What I also really like about this hotel, is that it is not in the hustle and bustle of town and it is reasonably priced.

Hollywood Celebrity Hotel
1775 Orchid Ave, Los Angeles, CA 90028

This unassuming and casual hotel is great if you are on a budget and don't expect a swimming pool or spa. It has elements of Art Deco style within the hotel design and this adds a very nice touch. It is only a five-minute stroll to the *walk of fame,* and an added bonus is the laundry room!

Ace Hotel
929 South Broadway, Los Angeles, CA 90015
1927 C. Howard Crane, Walker & Eisen

This hotel was built for the Maverick film studio, along with the theatre and tower which now represent the 'maverick' film stars.

It was Mary Pickford, Douglas Fairbanks Sr, along with Charlie Chaplin and D.W. Griffith who lead the way in forming the United Artists Studio and this hotel and theatre are the result. At the time it was the tallest building in LA and is an architectural treasure. The theatre is adorned with Spanish spires and ornate wood and stone work as Mary Pickford was deeply impressed with Spanish castles and cathedrals.

It has stayed mostly true to its roots over the years, and in 2014 the hotel and theatre reopened, after a full restoration programme. The hotel has intricate detailing of stone work on the facade and the vertical spandrels and tower dominates the surrounding buildings. It has a rooftop bar and swimming pool where the stonework can be fully appreciated. All in all, this hotel and theatre are not to be missed when staying in LA.

Carlyle Inn
119 South Robertson Blvd, Los Angeles, CA 90035

The hotel can boast of many elements that have been taken from Art Deco design in its curvilinear detailing and colour scheme.

It has 32 well equipped guest rooms and is reasonably priced.

Best Western Plus Hollywood Hills Hotel
6141 Franklin Ave, Hollywood, CA 90028

This retro style hotel is great if you are watching the purse strings. The modernist design and functionality are superb. It is close enough to the attractions and has all the amenities you could wish for including a swimming pool.

Georgian Hotel
1415 Ocean Ave, Santa Monica, CA 90401
1933

This colourful Art Deco hotel offers a dalliance with the old Hollywood style. It is impeccably decorated and furnished in keeping with the ethos of the hotel and the service matches.

The rooms are all comparable the only difference is the aspect you require. The ocean view from the high floors is worth the extra price.

OUT & ABOUT

The Know Where Bar
5634 Hollywood Blvd, Los Angeles, CA 90028

This cocktail bar is the epitome of the prohibition speakeasy. The owner Ben Adams along with Alex Meza have recreated Ben's Grandfathers bar, which proudly stood in Chicago back in the 1960s. This bar has Ben's own personal touches and his attention to detail does not go missed. Particularly nice is the vinyl music. The velvet furnishings add to the glamour and the classic cocktail list is very welcoming.

Cascade Theatre
1731 Market St, Redding, CA 96001
1934-5 J. Lloyd Conrich

The exterior of this cinema displays an impressive cast concrete frieze depicting north state industry. It was closed in 1997 and reopened in 2004 after a restoration project. The cinema has a seating capacity of 1000.

Alex Theatre Performing Arts & Entertainment Center
216 N Brand Blvd, Glendale, CA 91206
1925 Lindley & Selkirk Associates

It was in 1940 that *S.Charles Lee* was commissioned to redesign the exterior of this building that included the impressive 100ft tall column with neon lights topped with a spiked neon sphere, which gave it a starburst appearance. This venue has a striking Egyptian appearance. It was added to the NRHP list in 1996 and has one screen with a seating capacity of 1381.

Catalina Casino
1 Casino Way, Avalon, CA 90704
1929 Walter Webber & Summer Spauling

The new Catalina Casino was opened after a refurbishment programme costing $2 million. Serving as a theatre on the main floor and promenade and ballroom on the upper level this building had a height equal to a 12-storey structure.

The first level cinema has a seating capacity of 1,154 and a massive single screen with the added attraction of its original 4-manual, 16 rank pipe organ built by the Page Organ Company of Ohio.

Black Cat Tavern
3909 Sunset Blvd, Los Angeles. CA 90029
1939 *Frank L. Stiff*

In 1966 this bar was established as a local LGBT tavern and it was on New Year's Eve of that year that LAPD infiltrated the bar with many arrests taking place.

In 1967 the first demonstrations protesting against police harassment of LGBT people took place here preceding the Stonewall riots by over two years. The gastropub bar has an Art Deco facade and an interior that fits very well with its origins.

Bullocks Wilshire (The Parkinsons)
3050 Wilshire Blvd, Los Angeles. CA 90005
1930 John & Donald Parkinson

This 230,000 square-foot building was designed as a luxury department store for John G.

Bullock and it wasn't until 1989 that the store was incorporated into the Macey chain. The exterior has an impressive 241-foot tower whose top has a tarnished green copper sheath.

Part of the interior design includes a ceiling mural of the porte-cochere painted by *Herman Sachs*. In its heyday the store served the upper crust of Los Angeles society and patrons include John Wayne, Greta Garbo Walt Disney to name but a few. The building was listed on NRHP in 1978 and in 1994 was acquired by the Southwester Law School who restored and adapted the internal structure to suit their needs.

Burbank City Hall
275 E Olive Avenue, Burbank, CA 91502
1943 *William Allen & George Lutzi*

The site of municipal government for Burbank and has been on the listed building register (NRHP) since 1996.

The main lobby tower is 77 feet in height and features twenty different types of marble in its Art Deco detailing. It has several bas-reliefs and sculptured panels mainly attributed to *Bartolo Mako* but its most notable feature are the large murals by *Hugo Ballin*. 'The Four Freedoms' and 'Burbank Industry' can be found in the Council Chamber and in the rotunda.

El Rey Theatre
5515 Wilshire Blvd, Los Angeles, CA 90036
1936-37 Clifford A. Balch

In the mid-1980s this venue closed and reopened hosting concerts and live events with a seating capacity of 900. It is located in the area known as the Miracle Mile of Los Angeles due to the preserved Art Deco buildings. The building is unmissable with its neon lighting, sweeping staircase and grand ballroom.

Film Exchange Building
6424 Santa Monica Blvd, Los Angeles. CA 90038
1937

This three-story brick and concrete building were once home to the Afga Ansco film making industry. Because the manufacture of film materials was highly flammable the building was constructed to solid specifications. It is now an office space and it still features its high ceiling and ornate exterior panel detailing.

Regency Bruin Theatre
961 Broxton Avenue, Los Angeles. CA 90024
1937 *Simeon Charles Lee*

Originally opened by Fox West Theatres it had 876 seats all on a single floor.

It has a wrap-around marquee that is visible from all four roads that intersect at the theatre. The original theatre had painted luminous stencils which glowed in the dark but sadly these have been long painted over. The Regency company took over in 2010 and the seating capacity is listed as 696.

Good Ship Grace
2432 Hyperion Ave, Silver Lake, Los Angeles, CA
1941

This nautical theme two storey building resembling a ship was the former recording studio for Haven of Rest Ministries. It was given its name as the original

Christian quartet formed in 1934 of the crew of the Good Ship Grace, commissioned the building. No architect has been found for the building despite research by past and present owners of the building.

Grand Central Air Terminal
1310 Glendale Airway, Glendale, CA
1928

This was the first major airport in the Los Angeles area, and it opened for passenger service in 1928. In 1959 the airport closed as it was too small for operating the larger jetliners. All that remains now is the Grand Central Air Terminal and plans are afoot to transform the area into a visitor attraction after a sympathetic restoration programme. It has been owned by the Disney Corporation since 1997.

Wiltern Theatre
2790 Wilshire Blvd, Los Angeles, CA 90010
1931 Stiles O. Clements, of Morgan, Walls & Clements

This is one of the largest venues in LA, with a variety of concerts and special events throughout the year. It adjoins the twelve storey Art Deco landmark of the Pellissier building, with its distinctive blue tiled facade. The entire complex is normally referred to as the Wiltern Centre. The interior of the theatre was designed by *G. Albert Lansburgh* featuring opulent murals, gold leaf and the exuberant suspended sunburst from the ceiling.

The Edison
108 W. 2nd Street 100, Los Angeles, CA 90012

This opulent and decadent nightclub and bar opened in 2007 and is situated in a transformed power plant building. It has proved a crowd pleaser and the venue in the Higgins building basement, has an exciting programme of events themed around the prohibition era throughout the year.

Dresden Restaurant
1760 N. Vermont Ave, Los Angeles, CA 90027

This restaurant is a throwback to yesteryear and a real nostalgia trip. The nightly live jazz in the lounge is a great attraction not to miss.

Union Station
800 N. Alameda St, Los Angeles, CA 90012
1939 J & D.B. Parkinson

Half a million people attended the grand opening of this train station on its completion in 1939. The architecture is

a combination of Spanish Colonial Revival and Art Deco styles. A monumental restoration programme was undertaken to restore this phenomenal building back to its glorious heyday. In addition to the full restorative works the former Harvey House restaurant that closed in

1967 has been reopened. Even if you are not travelling from this building it has to be on your list of places to visit!

Hollywood Pantages Theatre
6233 Hollywood Blvd, Los Angeles, CA 90028
1930 B. Marcus Prikeca

This theatre has a colourful history and was even acquired by Howard Huges in 1949 for his RKO theatre circuit. It has been home to the Oscars, and hosted all the main celebrities and shows over the decades. It has been fully renovated at the beginning of the twenty first century and has a capacity for over 2700. Be prepared to be dazzled!

The Eastern Columbia Building
849 S. Broadway, Downtown Los Angeles, CA 90014
1930 Claud Beelman

This landmark building is also referred to as the Eastern. The spectacular shade and design make it an unmissable and a beacon for miles around. It is a thirteen-story building that has been converted into condominiums.

Egyptian Theatre
6712 Hollywood Boulevard, Los Angeles, CA 90028
1922 Mendel Meyer & Philip W. Holler

This historic listed cinema was opened by *Sid Grauman* the great American entrepreneur and showman, five weeks prior to the discovery of King Tutankhamen's tomb by Howard

Carter, and the subsequent Egyptian Revival mania that ensued. It has had many highs and lows over the years and closed its doors in 1992, then following an earthquake in 1994, it was badly damaged. In 2013 it underwent a total renovation and the cinema is once again thriving.

The Old Santa Ana City Hall
217 North Main St, Santa Ana, CA 92701
1934-35 William Horace Austin Jr & Harold C. Wildman

The most striking feature of this building are the sculptures of two bearded guards that top the pilasters flanking the front entrance. The building can also boast details of ziggurats and chevrons with fine bas-reliefs under each window. It now houses commercial outlets.

San Diego County Administration Centre
1600 Pacific Hwy, San Diego, CA 92010
1938 W. Templeton Johnson, S.W. Hamill, R. Requa & L. J. Gill

This impressive building is in the Beaux-Arts/Spanish Revival style with its Art Deco elements. It houses the offices of the Government of SD County that was funded by the Works Progress Administration. It is 150 ft in height with 7 floors that include 2 basement levels. The WPA combination of styles include zig-zag moderne motifs along with the central office tower and smooth surfaced columns, overall it all sits well with the building.

HOLLYWOOD Sign
Mount Lee, Los Angeles, CA 90068

The iconic letters at Mount Lee have stood since 1923, it is 13.7m tall and 106.7m long. It is located on restricted property, however, a good view point and photo opportunity is from the Griffith Observatory (metro available). Alternatively, guided tours and horseback excursions to great vantage points are available.

COLORADO

Capital: Denver
Became the 38th State: 1876
Flower: Rocky Mountain Columbine
Fossil: Stegosaurus

COSGRIFF HOTEL and COURT — CRAIG, COLORADO

ACCOMMODATION

The Broodmoor
1 Lake Avenue, Colorado Springs, CO 80906
1918 Warren & Wetmore

This is not just a hotel but a whole holiday resort. It has an illustrious history which charts its many owners from Spencer Penrose who made his vast fortune in gold mining ore, processing and real estate; to the current owners and its many reinventions over time. During the 1930s it even had its own aircraft hangar to cater for its clientele who flew directly into the nearby airport of the Peterson Air & Space Museum, as it's called today.

It is a fully inclusive resort which really caters for all ages and tastes. Whether it be golf, swimming, or adventure trails, it's all here. You have the option of accommodation in the main impressive and imposing hotel with its decorative interior, which is very reminiscent of stepping back to the Edwardian era.

Despite the alterations and grand modifications, it still retains that buzz of excitement of the golden age. You can either stay in a beautiful suite with rich furnishings or a simpler but very comfortable room. Particularly nice are the suites on the higher floors in the tower rooms.

Courtesy of the Broodmoor Hotel

Magnolia Hotel
818 17th St, Denver, CO 80202
1911 Harry Edbrooke

After a four-year renovation programme this former First National Bank has opened as a luxurious hotel retaining its grandeur and opulence of yesteryear. It has many unique touches like the collection of vintage safety-deposit boxes

attached to the lobby wall paying homage to the building's roots. The Denver based company responsible for the refit Oz Architecture incorporated the authentic history of the building into the restoration programme. The original elevators, phone booths, brass light fixtures and the terracotta facade are highlights. Early twentieth design can be seen in the custom made carpeting and flamboyant Ballroom with it glass atrium ceiling. With many different types of guestrooms to choose from this is an extremely comfortable and opulent hotel.

Crawford Hotel
1702 Wynkoop Street, Denver, CO 80202

This station hotel, started life back in the late 1880s and has undergone many changes, but still retained that air and excitement of its heyday years, during the jazz age. It was in 1953, when the neon signs, adorning the exterior were erected. The Union station was revitalised at that time; however, it had not anticipated, the impact that the opening of a new nearby airport, would have on train travel, at the time.

THE
CRAWFORD
HOTEL
DENVER UNION STATION

The hotel with its 112 guest rooms still has the air and sophistication of the bygone years. Located on the second floor are the Pullman rooms, which are very much in keeping with the nostalgic train cabins of the past. They have custom made Art Deco furnishings and the design and layout of the rooms are in keeping with being on a Pullman. The rooms

are also designed to give you a view of the passing world, as if on an actual train. You can peer down for your glass walled entrance hallway into the restaurants of Denver Union Station and at the travellers passing by, on their journeys.

Once again, this hotel is very much in vogue and the impressive foyer and public areas are a time capsule back to the decadent spirited Art Deco era.

Oxford Hotel
1600 17th Street, Denver, CO 80202

This luxury hotel that opened in 1893 has a labyrinth of Art Deco styling throughout. The 80 guest rooms and suits are elegantly furnished with tiled bathrooms reminiscent of the 1930s.

The public areas are all a throwback to a bygone age and it has a great ambience both day and night.

Heister House
Salida, Colorado
1943 Elwood and Frances Heister

This Art Deco/moderne home was built in 1943 and is listed on the National Register of Historic Places. The features include original woodwork, lighting and design elements. It has three bedrooms with a maximum  capacity of six people. It is situated in a nice area with an adjacent park. Please see HomeAway website to book this property for short term vacation lets.

Courtesy of Homeaway.com

OUT & ABOUT

Lamar Theatre
219 South Main Street, Lamar, CO 8105
1946 Charles D. Strong

This venue was built by the Atlas Theatre Corporation. Charlie Yeager the owner hired a prominent Denver architect, *Charles D. Strong* to design the Lamar.

Some of the highlights and features that this special theatre/cinema has to offer are; the monolithic façade complete with its green terracotta and buff stucco. A ticket booth in aluminium with curved glass. It has the working original Aquarium, with colourful tropical fish.

You will find an impressive, proscenium in the auditorium. It also has mural panels in fluorescent colours which are black light activated and the pastel colour scheme with beautiful floral mural work.

Over the past twenty years it has had sympathetic renovations and restorations.

Glen Huntington Band Shell
Canyon Blvd, Boulder, CO 80302

The Glen Huntington Band Shell was built in 1938. It was designed by local architect *Glen Huntington*, and is situated in a designated park and is highly prized by locals.

Photo credit Roadarch.com

Boulder County Courthouse
Pearl Street, Boulder, CO
1933 Glen Huntington

This courthouse replaced a previous one from 1882, which was destroyed by fire. It is now used as county government offices.

It is constructed of sandstone in a stepping stone pattern and this was achieved to perfection by cleverly altering the dimensions of the stones, hence accentuating the pattern of the building's façade.

The attractive bas-relief above the buildings entrance depicts a miner with his pick and a farmer with his sickle and the rising sun behind them.

Peterson Air and Space Museum
150 Ent Avenue, Peterson AFB, CO 80914
1942

This air museum and former military and public airport is named after Lieutenant Edward J. Peterson a local pilot who gave his life during a training exercise in 1942. He was married to a fellow pilot and he was greatly admired for his dedication and commitment, by his fellow colleagues and superiors alike. Five months after his death his Daughter was born. This museum has many buildings and hangars and is where the Broadmoor Hotel guests would arrive and depart from. The airport even constructed a dedicated airplane hangar to be used by the guests and businessmen travelling to the resort.

Hugo Municipal Pool
Jct. of US 287 & 6th Avenue, Hugo, CO
Lloyd E Heggenberger

This attractive WPA swimming pool constructed in the popular Moderne style is listed on the National Register of Historic Places. It looks as fresh and vibrant today as it did 80 years ago.

Lakeside Amusement Park
4601 Sheridan Blvd, Denver, CO 80212

This family run amusement park, originally opened in 1908 and is opposite Lake Rhoda. It still has some original structures from the 1930s, however, the majority of structures were designed by *Richard Crowther* and built after he moved to Denver in 1948.

Buerger Brothers Building
1742 Champa St, Denver, CO 80202
1929 Montana Fallis updated 1937

This building is considered to be one of the finest examples of Art Deco in Colorado. It used to house the offices and distribution centre for the Buerger Brothers who were the western region's premier barber and beauty shop supply company. Today it is used for retail space and has 31 apartment lofts. It has a decorative and colourful tiled facade and its original signage.

Horace Mann Middle School
E Van Buren Street, Colorado Springs, CO 80907
1931 Temple Buell

The façade of this building displays the diversity and decorative aspects that Art Deco can behold. The brick work is advantageously used to add surface depth and ornamentation.

Mullen Building
19th Avenue, Denver, CO 80218
1933-36 Temple H. Buell

This is another master-piece from the architect
Temple Buell. The Mullen building was designed as
a dormitory for Nurses and it is a poignant building
at Buell was a patient at the hospital here with TB
prior to him designing this new building. He took his inspiration from many areas
including the Mayans/Aztecs and emulating their elaborate headdresses in the
masonry designs.

University Building
910 16th Street, Downtown Denver, CO 80202
1910 William E. & Arthur Addison Fisher

The University was originally built in 1911, as the A.C. Foster Building, and
renamed the University Building in 1929 when it also underwent an entrance
remodel and the inclusion of a large terracotta panel. It was listed on the National
Register of Historic Buildings in 1978. In 1980 after being sold to the University
Investment Company, it was fully renovated and restored. It has since changed
ownership, and has offices and commercial outlets.

Fire Department 11
40 West 2nd Avenue, Denver, CO 80223
1937

This is Denver's second oldest active fire station; it
was built with WPA funding. It has some impressive
Art Deco features not only in the overall brickwork
design but also the original signage.

Photo credits Jeremiah Herderich

Bryant Webster Elementary School
Quivas Street, Denver, CO 80211
1931 G Meredith & J Roger Musick

This interesting red brick building has many impressive Art Deco features, and is
well worth taking the time to visit the exterior. The central column and ornate
brickwork designs lend to an overall feel of a sacred place as it resembles a large
place for worship.

CONNECTICUT

Capital: Hartford
Became the 5th State: 1788
Nickname: Constitution State
Bird: American Robin

STRATFIELD HOTEL — BRIDGEPORT, CONN.

ACCOMMODATION

Water's Edge Resort and Spa
1525 Boston Post Road, Westbrook CT 06498

This beachfront resort is not Art Deco in design but was built in the 1920s and exudes that bygone era of escapism frivolity and fun. It was originally the summer home of a wealthy businessman from New York and when his income took a turn for the worse in 1940, he sold it to be transformed into this relaxed resort.

It has perfectly landscaped gardens and beautiful views of Long Island. You can easily imagine F. Scott Fitzgerald sauntering around this city refuge. It has been a magnate to many famous celebrities over the years.

It has 100 guest rooms in the main hotel all decorated in the New England style and 68 seaside villas. Along with the private beachfront it can boast of having two swimming pools.

OUT & ABOUT

O'Rourke Diner
728 Main Street, Middletown CT 06457

This famous diner has stood here since 1930 with various owners over the decades. Following a devastating fire in 2006 a fundraising campaign around the World led to its full renovation. Originally built by the Mountain View Diner Company it was in 1941 that John O'Rourke took over the business.

William R. Cotter Federal Building
135-149 High Street, Hartford CT 06103

This 1931 building was designed by Malmfeldt, Adams & Prentice and used to house the post office and courthouses.

After extensive restoration it now serves solely as Federal Offices. It was renovated during the 1960s and 70s and in 1981 it was listed to the National Register of Historic Places. The exterior combines different styles of Art Deco, neo classical and stripped classical, whilst the interior is true to Art Deco alone and is a spectacular space.

© *Historic Buildings of Connecticut*

The Garde Theatre
325 State Street, New London CT 06320

This movie house is owned by 'The Garde Arts Centre' a non-profit performing arts and cinema centre, serving south eastern Connecticut. The exterior and interior are both impressive, well worth a visit.

© *cinematreasures.org*

Polish National Home
60 Charter Oak Avenue, South of Downtown Hartford CT 06106

This distinctive Art Deco building houses an ethnic community support organization. It was designed by the Polish-American architect *Henry Ludorf* in 1930 and is a listed on the National Register of Historic Places.

Southern New England Telephone Company Administration Building
227 Church Street, Downtown New Haven CT 06510

This skyscraper is the former headquarters of the SNET Company. It was completed in 1938 and designed by Douglas Orr & Roy W. Foote and was the tallest building in the city until 1966. It is prized as New Haven's premier example of Art Deco with its Stony Creek pink granite façade. In 2004 it was converted into 142 luxury apartments with two storefronts and renamed 'The Eli'.

Bridgeport Main Post Office
120 Middle Street, Bridgeport CT 06602

This three-story Art Deco moderne style building was designed by Louis A. Simon and completed in 1934.

It features artwork funded by the department's section of painting and sculpture with murals in the lobby area by *Robert Lambdin* charting mail delivery through the ages.

City Arts on Pearl
233 Pearl Street, Bridgeport CT 06608

This 1927 Art Deco building is now home to numerous non-profit making organizations along with gallery space. The small and intimate theatre is located in the basement of the building and seats 195 people.

© *hartforddailyphoto*

Warner Theatre
68-82 Main Street, Torrington CT 06790

This very fine theatre opened in 1931 as part of the Warner Bros, chain of movie theatres. It was designed by *Thomas W. Lamb* nationally renowned for his elaborate designs.

Exhaustive fundraising brought it back to its former original glory. The attention to detail was not spared on any aspect of the restoration; even the 'monkey fur' wall covering (actually crushed velvet) was restored and resourced from a German supplier where necessary. The vivid blood orange colour brings the theatre alive. The original Art Deco patterned carpet has been meticulously recreated. The venue is now a major art performing centre.

© *cinematreasures.org*

75

DELAWARE

Capital: Dover
Became the 1st State: 1787
Fruit: Strawberry
Bird: Blue Hen

W-8   U. S. POST OFFICE, COURT HOUSE AND CUSTOM HOUSE, RODNEY SQUARE, WILMINGTON, DEL.

ACCOMMODATION

Hotel Rodney
142 2nd St, Lewes, DE 19958

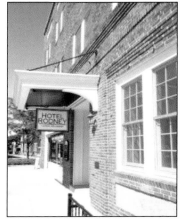

Originally built in 1926 this small boutique hotel offers 20 guest rooms and four suites over two floors.

The interior is particularly chic, as it is designed to reflect 1920s New York style. It is conveniently located near to restaurants and shops.

Hotel Du Pont
42 West 11th St, Wilmington, DE 19801

This historic hotel has been remodelled several times between 1908-1923 and is in the Italian Renaissance architectural style. However, during the Art Deco era it was the celebrated hotel of everyone who was anyone! The interior is luxurious, decadent and evocative of a bygone age, especially with the addition of the Gold Ballroom. Guestrooms and suites are elegantly furnished and the restaurants are first class.

OUT & ABOUT

F.W. Woolworth Building
839 N. Market St, Wilmington, DE
1940 H.W. Stakes

Lower Market Street is a Historic District in Wilmington, take a good wander around and you will be rewarded with varying architectural styles including Art Deco, Classical Revival, and Greek Revival. The Woolworth building was operated as a store until 1997 and it was added to the NRHP in 1987. It is now owned by BPG Property Group who lease it as a retail store. Its steel frame construction has a masonry curtain wall. The facade has alternating peach and cream vertical stripes of terracotta tiles with lotus motifs. On 9th street the grey medallion with the emblematic signage on the chamfered corner is a very fine view.

Max Keil Building
700 N. Market Street, DE
1938 H.M. Ballinger

Originally built in 1875, this three-story commercial building was modified in 1938. The front facade has a peach coloured terracotta wall and large rectangular display window. It was added to the NRHP in 1985.

Milton Theatre
110 Union St, Milton, DE 19968

Originally dating to c1905 and updated in 1939 this venue has been home to a plethora of variety acts, silent and talkie movies and musical entertainment. A local community theatre group have lovingly renovated and restored this building, it now has a wide variety of performances throughout the year, with a capacity of approx. 200 guests.

FLORIDA

Capital: Montgomery
Became the 22nd State: 1819
Flower: Camellia
Bird: Yellowhammer

Miami lies on the south east side of the Florida Peninsula, separated from the Atlantic Ocean by the Biscayne Bay lagoon and Miami Beach.

Miami Beach is a separate municipality from Miami and is located on an island; which is connected to the mainland by a series of bridges. It is World famous for its comprehensive Art Deco District, of which we have mainly Barbara Baer Capitman (1920-1990) to thank (hence the size of this section in the book), for its existence. Due to this admiral lady and her hard and long campaigning over the years, to save the Art Deco district from the bulldozers, the majority of the legacy

she left behind is now protected for future generations. You can see a tribute to this heroic lady in the 74-acre Lummus public park on 13th Street, near to the Cordozo Hotel, which was the first hotel to be restored. The bronze memorial was created when she was 19 years old, by her Sculptor mother, Myrtle Bachrach Baer and was initially completed in 1939.

The Art Deco district is located in the heart of South Beach from 6th Street to 23rd Street and rose following the Great Miami Hurricane of 1926.

Miami Beach is the largest twentieth century Architectural historic district in the States and has been listed on the National Register of Historic Places since 1979.

© Tom Hollyman MDPL

It features more than nine hundred historic buildings most of these were completed in the 1920s and 1930s. The majority of these historic buildings are Art Deco in style; however, some are in the Mediterranean Revival, Miami Modern (MiMo) or Vernacular style. The Streamline Moderne buildings that are less ornate in design coincides and reflects the stripped back times after the stock market crash and the Great Depression.

The Miami Architects took a new slant on the design and decoration of the buildings creating what we refer to now as Tropical Deco (originally most

Mural by Earl La Pan in the foyer of the Essex Hotel

buildings were painted white, the pastel shades were added during later decades). The imagery of playful ornamentation, ocean liner motifs and colour, made Miami Beach what it is today.

Close up of the mural by Earl La Pan in the Victor Hotel

Walk inside the Victor Hotel or the Essex House and you'll find murals evoking scenes of the Everglades, terrazzo flooring, chandeliers and glass blocks.

You may notice that many of South Beach's hotels signage has two names on the façade for instance the SLS and the Ritz Plaza or the Ritz-Carlton and DiLido Beach. As another measure to preserve the original architecture of these buildings, the original name on the façade must also remain.

The district comprises of municipal buildings, shops and many hotels in subtle pastel shades, often referred to as 'tropical deco'. The styles of the buildings vary greatly from Streamline Moderne to the more classic vernacular Art Deco.

Ocean Drive is a section located along the oceanfront and has a spectacular array of Art Deco buildings. Collins Avenue (State Road A1A) is located one block inland and parallels Ocean Drive. It is Collins Avenue, that joins the numerous neighbourhoods together, here you will also find an abundance of Art Deco on offer.

Like all the hotels and buildings in this guide book, it is needless to say that the interior decoration does not always reflect the exterior and vice versa, so please check further prior to booking, so that your expectations can be met.

ACCOMMODATION

I recommend that when you check in at a hotel, take a look at your room and decide if you want to go for an upgrade, if available. From experience it can be that the standard room is still in original furnishings and the suites etc. have been updated to more modern contemporary, so you never quite know what is in store for you.

So, don't be afraid to ask for a room change either upscale or downscale! Not everyone at the hotel is specifically there for the Art Deco, so you may be surprised with what you find in other rooms. You may not want a sea view, so check out the rooms with views to the Art Deco buildings that surround the hotel.

I highly recommend taking a guided tour of the area by the knowledgeable staff of the Miami Design Preservation League; 1001 Ocean Drive, Miami Beach, FL 33139, they really are worth their weight in gold! These can be booked online or directly through the majority of hotels.

Also remember that you can hotel hop, to experience several hotels. If this doesn't appeal to you, make sure that you experience either, lunch, dinner or evening drinks, in the other hotels to experience the interior.

With dozens of hotels to choose from, I have represented some of the noteworthy large and small places to stay in. Make sure you allow yourself enough time to explore and fully appreciate the remarkable surroundings of the Art Deco district and all that it has on offer.

The hard decision now, is to choose which hotel, or hotels to spend the night in!

National Hotel

1677 Collins Avenue, Miami Beach FL 33139
1939 Roy France

This iconic hotel was fully renovated in 2014 and the flavour of Art Deco furnishings can be seen throughout the hotel. It has 152 guest rooms in total, hence being mid-range in size. The deluxe poolside cabana rooms make up 36 suites, with the 116 rooms in the main building. They mainly have custom made Art Deco style and contemporary furnishings in the suites and the penthouse. The hotel is also known for having the longest pool in Miami Beach of 205ft, and is resplendently lined with palm trees.

Look out for the original oak bar centre piece of the Blues Bar and the fully restored carpeting and chandelier in the ballroom and oval room. Particularly striking, is the intricate ceiling mosaic in the restaurant, consisting of thousands of tiny tiles. The mosaic is in honour of a frequent patron to the hotel, that of the Art Deco artist Tamara de Lempicka (1898-1980). The image is after her painting of 1921 entitled 'Girl with Gloves', she is such an interesting and captivating artist and most famous for her paintings produced during the Art Deco period.

.

TAMARA'S BISTRO

Waldorf Towers
860 Ocean Drive, Miami Beach FL 33139
1937 Albert Anis

This small hotel with 44 guest rooms is located at the heart of all the action. The ocean view deluxe room is well worth the extra, like with all the majority of hotels, an upgrade usually pays off with the view and space gained.

The restaurant is great for 'people watching' and the staff are very friendly and obliging. The quirky tower adds a new dimension to this ascetically pleasing hotel.

Cardozo
1300 Ocean Drive, Miami Beach FL 33139
1939 Henry Hohauser

This famous iconic hotel has recently reopened after a multi-million-dollar refurbishment and is owned by Gloria and Emilio Estefan. The interior is impeccable

with minimalist rooms and relaxation the key factors. The hotel does not have an interior restaurant, however, the *Larios on the Beach* restaurant owned by the Estefan's is the desired choice that compliments well with its Latin orientated menu.

Pestana South Beach Hotel
1817 James Avenue, Miami Beach FL 33139
1952 Gerard Pitt

The style of this hotel is called Miami Modern (MiMo) which incorporates the classic (vernacular) and streamline deco. It is made up of four buildings with 97 guest rooms and suites. It gleams with its iconic Art Deco white and blue facades. It is nicely situated in the middle of Miami Beach seafront. Particularly appealing is the heated  indoor swimming pool around a neatly fashioned courtyard, should prefer to take a dip sand free!

The Hotel
801 Collins Avenue, Miami Beach FL 33139
1939 L. Murray Dixon

The Hotel, is formerly the Tiffany and consists of 53 guest rooms and suites. Following renovations and expansion, a new oceanfront addition has been added to The Hotel.

It comprises of 20 deluxe rooms, including two suites, which was completed in 2010. Located at 800 Ocean Drive, above the News Café, bringing The Hotel's rooms and suites down to the ocean is the other half. The two properties bring the total to 73 rooms and suites, with shared amenities.

The original building displays long thin porthole windows, along with glass block bands. This perfectly balances with the horizontal and vertical compositions, all executed in white.

The signage finial evokes the dirigible mooring mast originally at the top of the Empire State Building. It can also boast of having a welcoming rooftop pool.

SLS South Beach /Ritz Plaza Hotel
1701 Collins Avenue, Miami Beach, FL 33139
1940 L. Murray Dixon

This mini deco skyscraper hotel, pierces the sky with a fantasy smokestack. Following a complete renovation of the property in 2011, it opened as SLS South Beach hotel.

It has 115 guest rooms and suites and the style is one of soothing and crisp whites, accompanied by soothing harmonious furnishings. It has a lively swimming pool and lounging area.

Ritz Carlton Hotel
I Lincoln Road, Miami Beach Florida 33139
1953 Morris Lapidus

This hotel is a fine example of post modernism design. It has 375 luxurious guest rooms, including two poolside lanai wings. If you want to sample the design style and aesthetic of Lapidus you will find it here. The interior has been cleverly maintained in a contemporary Art Deco/modernist style.

The Ritz Carlton Oceanview Suite
luxurious and decadent

Albion Hotel
1650 James Avenue, Miami FL 33139
1939 Polevitsky & Russell

This is a seven-story streamline hotel, resembles an ocean liner; with horizontal bands, rounded corners and portholes with an upper bridge.

This theme has been used on other hotels on Miami Beach and works exceedingly well. The public areas are nicely furnished in Art Deco style. It has 100 guest rooms and a swimming pool.

Beacon South Beach Hotel
720 Ocean Drive, Miami FL 33139
Henry O. Nelson, 1936

The façade of this hotel is made up of horizontal and vertical banding, triangle and half circles which extend down from the parapet. Above the first floor you can see openings that are stylized plant designs. It has 75 guest rooms and an airy semi-circular open plan foyer with decorative railing and terrazzo floor.

Berkeley Shore Hotel
1610 Collins Avenue, Miami FL 33139
1940 architect Albert Anis

The Berkeley Shore, now features twice as many rooms as the original hotel. It is now

part of Iberostar and underwent a multimillion-pound renovation and expansion with an adjacent ten storey tower.

The glorious façade with its decorative half-circled finales combines Streamline Moderne with the ornate Art Deco design.

The round central shaft rises above the front foyer marquee; up through the upper two floors and forms a banded tower, like a corkscrew at the top.   Like most of the hotels it has a contemporary modern interior. It has 96 guest rooms and a swimming pool.

Raleigh Hotel
1775 Collins Avenue, Miami Beach FL 33139
1940   L. Murray Dixon

This iconic hotel is currently under restoration and renovation. It features a cubist façade with an impeccable marble and tiled reception/lobby. It also has one of the most photographed swimming pools in Miami Beach, as it is in the shape of Sir Walter Raleigh's coat of arms. A beautiful garden has been created by designers showcasing exhibitions until the hotel is opened later in 2020.

Cavalier Hotel
1320 Ocean Drive, Miami Beach FL 33139
1936 Roy F. France

This striking hotel is located near to Lummus Park. It was fully renovated in 2015, and the interior is combination of contemporary and quirky. The Cavalier Hotel maintains its original exterior facade of bright pastel colours in Mayan

designs and it also looks striking when lit up in the evening. The interior of the hotel is designed to be show stopping in a bourgeoisie French/deco style. The 46 guest rooms are all distinctively decorated in wood with Chicago brick walls.

Hotel Astor
956 Washington Avenue, Miami Beach FL 33139
1936 T. Hunter Henderson

This understated sleek chic hotel has 42 minimalist guest rooms and suites, all redecorated in 2016. If you really want to splash the boat out, you can stay in the Astor Suite which has its own private terrace and gargantuan marble bathroom to sip your champagne.

Colony Hotel
736 Ocean Drive, Miami Beach FL 33139
1936 Henry Hohauser

This hotel was one of the first in the Tropical Deco style by this prolific and imaginative architect. The lobby features a wealth of mint green vitrolite and a deco style mural over the fireplace. The blue neon exterior is spectacular night and day. The interior is bright and

modern and described as European style decorated in furnishings which complement the Art Deco heritage with an accent to Europe with pine floors with a contemporary flair.

It has 48 guest rooms and the ocean front suites are worth that little extra, but remember you will invariably get extra noise. However, in the case of the Miami Beach location, it somehow adds to the overall vibe of the place.

The Marlin Hotel
1200 Collins Avenue, Miami Beach FL 33139
1939 L. Murray Dixon

This three-story hotel has 33 guest rooms and suites along with the award-winning restaurant of Osteria Del Teatro. It is located next to the shopping, nightlife and entertainment area.

Shepley Hotel
1340 Collins Avenue, South Beach Miami FL 33139
1938 Henry Hohauser

Revamped in 2013 by the Argentinian designer Pablo Chiappori the Shepley is elegant with nods to Art Deco in its interior. The 29 guest rooms are stylish in design and the exterior of the property will not disappoint.

Carlyle Hotel
1250 Ocean Drive, Miami FL 33139
1939 Kiehnel & Elliott

This hotel is made up of individual apartments/condos that are hired out via a rental agency. It is available online and booked the same way as a hotel. The apartments are large and airy and include a kitchen.

Typical of the architectural style of the buildings in the area this property has three recessed vertical towers which have semi-circular canopies located near the top. The curved corners add to the overall aesthetics of this pleasing building. It has been utilised as a filmset for Scarface and numerous other high-profile movies over the years.

Dream South Beach Hotel (The Tudor & Palmer House)
1111 Collins Avenue, Miami Beach FL 33139
1939 L. Murray Dixon

This hotel certainly lives up to its name with its first-class facilities. It has the *Naked Taco* Mexican restaurant, and on the rooftop, you will find the *High bar* with an infinity pool. The 108 modern contemporary guest rooms are equipped with a sitting area and a dining area. The adjacent Tudor and Palmer hotels both designed by L. Murray Dixon in 1939 have been meticulously renovated and joined the Dream Hotel. Along with the Kent Hotel adjacent to the Palmer House on the north, the three hotels form one of the strongest ensembles in the Art Deco district.

Essex House Hotel

1001 Collins Avenue, Miami Beach FL 33139
1938 Henry Hohauser

This Streamline Moderne landmark hotel is a historic South Beach gem, centrally located within steps of the clear blue Atlantic Ocean. The stylish, 70 guest room property includes 14 suites.

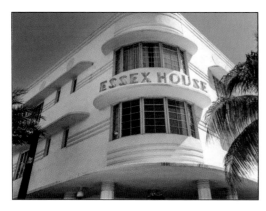

Features a small swimming pool and a relaxing terrace featuring Zen Sai, the hotel's signature Asian-fusion style restaurant. Essex House provides a unique vacation experience that allows guests to explore South Beach treasures and capture a piece of Miami Beach history.

An impressive mural by the self-taught artist Earl La Pan adorns the main lobby/lounge area.

The Tides
1220 Ocean Drive, Miami Beach FL 33139
1936 L. Murray Dixon

This hotel was the first to offer an
elevator in Miami and it was a favourite
place of Marilyn Monroe in the 1950s. It
was badly damaged by hurricane Irma and reopened 2018. It offers a top of the
range service with a glamorous interior that is evident in all the rooms, suites and
public areas. It has an outdoor pool.

Hotel Victor
1144 Ocean Drive, Miami Beach FL 33139
1936 L Murray Dixon

This hotel was fully restored and updated in
2013 and its iconic neon lit exterior is visible
from far afield. It has 91 guest rooms, a
restaurant and swimming pool. A feature of
the exterior are the round porthole windows
and long horizontal windows.

Congress Hotel-Condo
1052 Ocean Drive, Miami Beach FL 33139
1934 Henry Hohouser

This hotel-condo has 40 guest rooms and modern suites with kitchens, a rooftop pool and bar. It offers ocean front dining and rooms with spectacular views.

Kent Hotel
1131 Collins Avenue, Miami Beach FL 33139
1939 L. Murray Dixon

The dramatic exterior of the Kent Hotel is hard to miss. It has 60 guest rooms all decorated in fresh and contemporary modern styling. This small boutique hotel has an ambience of 1930s in a tranquil and informal setting, and it belongs to the hotel consortium Dream South beach.

Crescent Hotel
1420 Ocean Drive, Miami Beach FL 33139
1938 Henry Hohauser

This small 25 roomed hotel offers unfussy suites with full kitchens and whirlpool tubs plus a rooftop terrace. The reception area displays authentic terrazzo flooring and deco furnishings.

Leslie Hotel
1244 Ocean Drive, Miami Beach FL 33139
1937 Albert Anis

This iconic Art Deco hotel has 35 guestrooms. Its bright yellow and white façade is very welcoming. It has an attractive deco lobby and contemporary modern rooms. The Ocean view suites  are superb and like many of the hotels listed it offers big discounts for early bookings.

Delano Hotel
1685 Collins Avenue, South Beach Miami FL 33139
1947 Robert Swartburg

This impressive modernist building with
its central fin war fully renovated in 1994.
The 194 guest rooms and suites are first
class. The interior design is minimalist in
fresh light shades with a profusion of
white and striking deco designs rugs. The
swimming pool is most inviting and the
restaurant and bar receive top marks for
glamour and glitz.

The Whitelaw Hotel
808 Collins Avenue, Miami Beach FL 33139
1936 Albert Anis

This hotel offers 49 guest rooms that
are eclectically furnished and these
include marble bathrooms. A rooftop
sundeck and bar are always a
welcoming sight and this hotel has an
intimate feel about it despite its mid-
range sizing.

Nassau Suite Hotel
1414 Collins Avenue, Miami Beach FL 3313
Constructed 1936-37

This privately owned hotel offers 22 large guest suites with full kitchens and a complimentary breakfast. It has a personal and exclusive feel about it with its own private movie theatre, for guests.

Chesterfield Hotel & Suites
855 Collins Avenue, Miami Beach FL 33139
1938 Albert Anis

The hotel is the formulated by the merge of the 92 rooms Lily, Leon and Chesterfield hotel. It originally started out as the Helmor Hotel in 1938. It consists of 92 guest rooms with soaking tubs. It has a vibrancy with its rooftop bar and yoga studio. The guest rooms and suites have quality furnishings some are Mahogany with aluminium that complement the hardwood flooring.

Island House
1428 Collins Avenue, Miami Beach FL 33139
1949 Herbert Mathes

This family orientated property offers 20 guest rooms. The suites and studios are simply furnished and is ideal for families being laid back and casual.

Hotel Breakwater
940 Ocean Drive, South Beach Miami FL 33139
Anton Skislewicz, 1939

Hotel Breakwater is one of the most iconic hotels on Ocean Drive. It has been used as a backdrop to countless movies. It was restored and renovated in 2011 and has **99** guest rooms a slender terraced outdoor pool.

The white, yellow and blue façade is striking and it incorporates nautical motifs.

The rectangular symmetrical design of the hotel, crescendos with a spire; rising from the centre. The roofline follows a stepped ziggurat pattern. Particularly playful is the resemblance to a grand ocean liner ready to take on the Atlantic at any time!

Olsen Hotel Condo
7300 Ocean Terrace, Miami Beach FL 33141

This delightful Art Deco building was constructed in 1940. It used to be the Olsen Hotel, and has recently been renovated to a condo with 39 apartments over three floors. It is located at the North end of Miami Beach. It is in a great location if you are desire a quieter stay and it is a board walk away from the golden sands. The building is made up of residents and long-term rentals. This studio apartment is very reasonably priced accommodation and a minimum of 3 nights is required.

Pelican Hotel
826 Ocean Drive, Miami Beach FL 33139

This small boutique hotel was established in 1994, owned by Renzo Rosso of the Diesel Jeans company, it certainly is fun and quirky. The interior is the mastermind of Swedish designer *Magnus Ehrland.*

The 29 guest rooms and suites are all themed. The Art Deco styled rooms are 207 Deco(intreau), 307 Deco(ocktail) or 303 Executive thirties.

Room 303 Executive thirties   *Room 307 Deco(cktail)*

This hotel is popular so I recommend to book early so you can secure the room which most appeals to you!

Celino South Beach Hotel
640 Ocean Drive, Miami Beach, FL 33139
Henry Hohauser 1937

This hotel was updated and expanded in 2019 incorporating a beach front extension. The old merges well with the new and overall the aesthetics of the building are not overly compromised. The integrity of the original building is still intact and the tasteful refit is both modernist and in keeping. It has 132 guest rooms and suits, a courtyard bar and offers in-room dining. During its heyday regular clientele from the silver screen included Bogart and Rita Hayworth.

Winterhaven Hotel
1400 Ocean Drive, Miami Beach FL 33139
1939 Albert Anis

This hotel is set over six floors and has 70 well-appointed guest rooms.   The rooms feature Art Deco style and original furnishings. The lobby and light fitments are also Art Deco in design. The exterior design of the building is a Nautical theme.

Loews Hotel (formerly St. Moritz)
1601 Collins Avenue, Miami Beach FL 33139
Roy F. France 1939

This is a large hotel in comparison to many in the area with its 790 guest rooms. It was in 1998 that the property was fully restored and thankfully kept its iconic St Moritze tower. It has an outdoor pool and spa, along with fine dining and a sophisticated bar.

Ocean Surf Hotel

7436 Ocean Terrace, Miami Beach FL 33141

This hotel is located on the
north area of Miami beach and
has been newly renovated. The
exterior has porthole windows
and spacious balcony rooms. It
is located near to restaurants,
bars and shops. It offers casual
and stylish accommodation with
the beach on your doorstep.

OUT & ABOUT

Freedom Tower
600 North Biscayne Boulevard, Miami, FL 33132-1802

This is the most striking building on Biscayne Boulevard, in confectionary and architectural terms known as the "wedding-cake" style. Built in 1925, it is one of the oldest skyscrapers in south-eastern United States, and served for many years as the headquarters of the Miami Daily News.

Its name derives from its role as the immigration-processing centre for hundreds of thousands of Cuban refugees who arrived in the 1960's. Today it stands as a tribute to Cuban immigration

---

Tower Theatre
1508 SW 8th St, Miami, FL 33135

One of Miami's oldest cultural landmarks, Tower Theatre opened in 1926. The Art Deco movie house showcases a prominent 40-foot steel tower jutting from its neon marquee. During the 1950s and throughout the 1960s many Cuban refugees fled to Miami, and the area surrounding southwest Eighth Street was dubbed 'Calle Ocho', becoming a place of new beginnings for Cuban immigrants. Many Cuban families were introduced to the American culture through film at Tower Theatre. From 2002 Miami Dade College has managed the theatre operations. It offers comprehensive listings throughout the year, exhibitions and educational outreach programs.

404 Washington Avenue
Miami Beach FL 33139

Surprisingly this office building resembling a rocket or cylo was built in 1995 and designed by Bermillo & Associates. It sits exceedingly well in its Art Deco environment and is one of the most photographed buildings in Miami. It is located two blocks from the ocean and is bordered by 5th Street, Washington Avenue, 4th Street and Euclid avenue.

Art Deco Welcome Centre
1001 Ocean Drive, Miami Beach, FL 33139

Operated by the Miami Design Preservation League (MDPL) to promote, educate and preserve the Art Deco architecture in Miami. MDPL offer excellent daily guided walking tours of the Art Deco district which are informative and good value for money.

Sherbrooke Co-op
901 Collins Avenue, Miami Beach, FL 33139
1947 McKay & Gibbs

These private apartments/condos are set in an
impressive nautical Streamline Moderne style
building. Of particular note are the continuous
horizontal lines sweeping around the
curvilinear corner that rises like the prow of a
ship.

The Seymour
945 Pennsylvania Ave, Miami Beach, FL 33139

This building is now utilised as a local museum and community centre. It was
originally opened in 1936 as the Kingston Hall hotel. It has impressive original
features and a fully restored lobby. It is currently up for sale and possibly could
go full circle and return as a hotel.

Jewish Museum of Florida
301 Washington Ave, Miami Beach, FL 33139
1936 Henry Hohauser

The prolific architect *Henry Hohauser*
blended neo-classical and tropical Art
Deco motifs to create Miami Beach's
second synagogue. The synagogue was
converted into the Jewish Museum in
1993. The conversion retains many of
the original features, including the
balcony and bema (alter) while
providing space for changing
exhibits. Be sure to note the Star of
David superimposed on the Spandrel panels.

Wolfsonian Florida International University
1001 Washington Ave, Miami Beach, FL 33139

This Mediterranean style building was originally a
former storage facility and was designed by
Robertson and Patterson in 1927 with two stories

added in 1936 by
Robert Little. It was
converted to a
museum between
1987 and 1993 by
Mark Hampton.

The museum's full title is *Wolfsonian-FIU Museum of
Decorative and Propaganda Arts* and it covers the
period from 1885 to 1945 with an emphasis on
emergence of Modernity. Many of the objects are
donated from Mitchell Wolfson, Jr, who was an
advocate and collector of modernism and everyday

objects of the Art Deco period that are very much coveted today. The overall highlight of the museum has to be the 1929 Art Deco movie theatre marquee from Norristown, Pennsylvania at the rear of the entry hall.

United States Post Office
1300 Washington Ave, Miami Beach, FL 33119
1937 Howard L. Cheney

South Beach's Post Office reflects the austere, classically inspired institutional architecture which was popular in Europe in the late 1930s. The highlight of the interior is the mural by *Charles Hardman* depicting the meeting of the Spanish Conquistadors and the Native Americans, the two groups in battle, and the signing of a nominal treaty between the Native Americans and the US.

Senor Frog's
1450 Collins Ave, Miami Beach, FL 33139
1940 Henry Hohauser

Take a break at this restored diner
(formerly Jerry's Deli) another successful
design by the prolific architect Henry
Hohauser. It has such a pleasing curvilinear
and towered exterior. Pure joy!

Sterling Building
927 Lincoln Rd N, 200 Miami Beach, FL 33139

This local landmark is a 1941 Deco-Streamline renovation by *V.H. Nellenbogen* of a
1920s Mediterranean style building. At night the glass block façade glows with blue
light. The passage to the courtyard is faced in dyed polished keystone and features
a classic Tropical Art Deco terrazzo pattern.

Beach Patrol Headquarters
East end of 10th Street at Ocean Drive
c.1939

The beach patrol headquarters is a small streamline modern building depicting a ship. With its semi-circular bridge bordered by nautical railings and portholes on the first floor it playfully looks out to sea.

Bass Museum of Art
2100 Collins Avenue, Miami Beach, FL33139
1930 Russell T. Pancoast

Recognized as the first Tropical Art Deco edifice, the building opened in 1930 as the John Collins Memorial Library, designed by Collin's grandson, *Russell Pancoast*. A triptych of Miami's history is conveyed in the three relief panels over the entry portals. When the library moved out in 1962 the building became the Bass Museum of Art. It is clad entirely of keystone, the original building has been restored and a new wing was added in 2001.

Colony Theatre
1040 Lincoln Road, Miami Beach, FL 33139
1935 R.A. Benjamin

This theatre heralds the transitional style between the Mediterranean design of the 1920s and the Tropical Art Deco of the 1930s. It has pitched barrel tile roofs with stylized decoration and using modern materials displayed in the vitrolite glass. It has the seating capacity for 417 and a year-round list of events.

As you meander along the four mile stretch of boardwalk of Miami Beach you will see numerous colourful life guard stations. These individually designed huts started to appear in 1992 when a hurricane devastated all the existing non-descript ones. The combination of bright and pastel shaded cabins sit perfectly well alongside the hotel facades.

GEORGIA

Capital: Atlanta
Became the 4th State: 1788
Flower: Cherokee Rose
Fruit: Peach

Legion Park, Waycross, Ga.

ACCOMMODATION

Four Season Hotel
75 Fourteenth Street NE, Atlanta, GA 30309

It is interesting to that this International Style skyscraper was built in 1992. It is a throwback to the fusion of styles which swept through the USA during the 1930s and 1940s. The façade of rose and marble granite is spectacular and changes with the light of the day or evening. The hotel and interiors were designed by Hirsch Bedner Associates of Atlanta.

It has 244 guest rooms and suites in various styles. You will find on the 14th and 19th floors that the Midtown Deluxe Rooms are designed to be sleek and contemporary and best suit the Art Deco feel. Bar Margot is very much in the deco style as is the restaurant.

The Georgian Terrace Hotel
659 Peachtree St NE, Atlanta, GA 30308
1911 William Lee Stoddart

This hotel in the beaux arts style has 326 guest rooms and is elegantly furnished and refined throughout. The renowned and popular Livingston Restaurant and

Bar has a glamorous Art Deco style interior.

It has a rooftop pool and cafe, and one of the hotels claim to fame is that it hosted the premiere gala for the release of the film '*Gone with the Wind*' in 1939. It is conveniently located across the street from the Fox theatre.

OUT & ABOUT

Hartsfield-Jackson Atlanta Airport
6000 North Terminal Parkway, Atlanta, GA 30320
1940

Originally a racetrack in 1925, the land was then leased as an airfield. First it was called Candler Field after the former landowner, then four years later the city of Atlanta bought the land and the Atlanta Municipal Airport was born.

In the 1940s Delta Air Lines moved their company headquarters to the location. The Delta Flight Museum is situated next to the airport and is a worthy day out.

Suwanee City Hall
330 Town Center Avenue, Suwanee GA 30024
2009 BRPH of Marietta

© *Turner Construction*

This large civic building covers 24,000 square foot and has an impressive glass front and a 103-foot clock tower. It was designed in the Art Deco style and sits majestically amidst the town park.

The interior is more contemporary modern, the double set of stairs leading to the first floor are cleverly designed encapsulating an overall feeling of light and airy openness.

The Buckhead Diner
3073 Piedmont Road NE, Atlanta, GA 30305

This retro American diner has a real air of 1930s Art Deco. The exterior is as shiny as it gets with streamlined aluminium surfaces and neon signage.

Inside it is a show stopping mix of diner meets deco opulence with beautiful lighting and seating cubicles.

Fox Theatre
660 Peachtree St NE, Atlanta, GA 30308
1929 Oliver J. Vinour

This extravagant theatre was originally planned to be part of a large shrine temple; however, it was developed into this extraordinary theatre and movie venue. It has a distinctive design where Ancient Egyptian, Islamic, and Moorish architecture are interwoven.

After its fall and decline over the years, it has been resurrected, fully restored and now a top venue in the USA for hosting events throughout the year. The large auditorium seats over 4,600 guests and has played host to many famous celebrities including Elvis Presley.

Atlanta Municipal Auditorium

High Museum of Art
1280 Peachtree St NE, Atlanta, GA 30309
1983 Richard Meier

This contentious Streamline Moderne building that *Meier* designed, opening in 1983 seriously lacked display areas. Despite its large floor space of 135,000 sq ft, only 52,000 sq ft could be utilised as gallery space.

In 2005, three new buildings were designed by *Renzo Piano* and they have increased the volume of exhibits. The buildings fit perfectly with 1930s modernism aesthetic, the white concrete construction and grand atrium are works of art in themselves.

Majestic Diner
1031 ponce De Leon Ave NE, Atlanta, GA 30306

This Streamline Moderne diner has been operating since 1929. The red seated interior and neon strip signage lighting have been updated over the years. It is open 24/7 and serves a hearty breakfast, lunch and dinner.

Martin Luther King Jr.
Federal Building, 77 Forsyth St SW, Atlanta GA 30303
1933 A. Ten Eyck Brown

This building was constructed by the WPA for the United States Postal Service. It was a mail sorting office utilising its location adjacent to the terminal station and mail was transferred via tunnels from the railroad network. It later became a Federal Building and was renamed in 1988, it underwent a full renovation programme in 2012.

Olympia Building
23 Peachtree St, Atlanta, GA 30303
1936 E. Ivey & L. Crook

Located in the downtown area of Five Points district is the iconic Olympia Building. This two-storey building started a restoration programme in 2015. It has a marble and terracotta facade. The metal canopy has been reconstructed from historic images. It is also known for the flashing Coca-Cola sign that stands on top of the building a much later addition from 2003. The building is a retail outlet.

Plaza Theatre
1049 Ponce De Leon Ave NE, Atlanta, GA 30306
1939 George Harwell Bond

This theatre and movie palace have had a colourful history. With several owners over the decades, it was in the 1970s that it became an X-rated cinema and burlesque theatre. In 1983 the new owner converted the balcony area into a second auditorium. During the 2000s it became a non-profit organization. In 2017 the theatre was sold to the Executive Director of the Atlanta Film Society, Christopher Escobar.

HAWAII

Capital: Honolulu
Became the 50th State: 1959
Flower: Yellow Hibiscus
Marine Mammal: Humpback Whale

H - 271 Aloha Tower, Honolulu

ACCOMMODATION

The Royal Hawaiian Hotel
2259 Kalakaua Avenue, Honolulu HI 96815
1927

When this hotel was built, luxurious travel was top of the list, for all those who could afford it. A popular architectural style of the time was the Spanish Moorish

design, influenced and popularised by the screen star Rudolf Valentino. The hotel It is known as the pink palace, and certainly lives up to this name. It conjures up the exoticism and luxury along with extravagance of the Art Deco period.

Over the years it has been further developed with a new tower and further buildings. However, the main focus of the hotel will

always be the original building which has been fully preserved. The hotel can also lay claim, to the fact that the Aviator Sir Charles Kingsford Smith stayed here during his successful trans Pacific flight in 1928. The guest rooms and suites all carry through the exotic theme with rich furnishings and textiles.

OUT & ABOUT

Hawaii Theatre
1130 Bethel St, Honolulu, HI 96813
1922 W. Emory & M. Webb

This building is considered to be the premier example of Art Deco in Hawaii. It was the Consolidated Amusement Company formed by the entrepreneur Joel C. Cohen and John H. Magoon in 1913 who commissioned the building, contracting the local architects. It has seen many decades of entertaining until it desperately needed a major interior and exterior renovation programme. After the two phases were complete it reopened in 2004 at a cost of 32 million dollars. It is run as a non-profit corporation and seats 1,350 and is listed on the NRHP.

Central Fire Station
104 S. Berentania St, Honolulu, Hi 96813
1934 C.W. Dickey

Located near to the China town region of Honolulu you will find this impressive fire station. The geometric design on the large aluminium doors is striking complemented by the banded windows. It is listed on the NRHP.

Eugene Savagean (1883-1978) an American painter and sculptor was famous amongst other things for his Art Deco style murals. Some of his most impressive celebrate the lush and plentiful environment in his series of murals titled 'Festival of the Sea'. These were subject to a spectacular exhibition in 2015, at Honolulu Museum of Art, celebrating the Art Deco artist and buildings. This museum was established in 1922 and has an impressive collection of permanent and touring exhibitions.

IDAHO

Capital: Boise
Became the 43rd State: 1890
Vegetable: Potato
Horse: Appaloosa

Chief Motel and Service Station
24 Modern Rooms — Junction 89 and 30 N. — Montpelier, Idaho — Phone 6
ROYAL D. CLARK & SONS, Owners

ACCOMMODATION

Lava Hot Springs Inn
1 Center Street, Lava Hot Springs ID 83246
c.1920

This interesting building is situated next to the Portneuf river with its natural lava hot springs, and when it opened in the 1920s it was a hospital. The hotels aim is to maintain the look and feel of the original era, with adding some extra home comforts in its 17 guestrooms.

There is a choice of accommodation and treatments available at the spa. The hot pools are also open to the public and the town centre is within walking distance of the hotel.

OUT & ABOUT

Hoff Building
800 W Bannock St, Boise ID 83702
1930 Frank Hummel

Originally this building was the magnificent Hotel Boise that entertained and welcomed Presidents and the hoi polloi of its day. It unfortunately fell into disrepair and in 1976 it was bought by the Hoff Company, renamed and repurposed into office space.

Many of the original Art Deco features were lost. In 1978 and 1983 it changed hands twice and a restoration programme to install original Art Deco features was put in place. It has reintroduced the beauty that was lost, however, still maintains to have its resident ghost that frequents the 11th floor and Crystal Ballroom.

Bear Lake Middle School
633 Washington St, Montpelier ID 83254
1937 Frank H. Paradice

The exterior of this school has hardly changed over the years and is a fine hybrid of styles Spanish Revival, Modernist and Art Deco.

The architect *Frank Paradice* was renowned for his terracotta ornamentation and this building highlights this with its brick faced spandrels leading up to stylized floral and sun ray motifs above the main entrance.

Boise Municipal South Pool
921 Shoshone St, Boise ID 83705

This Lido has an interesting Art Deco entrance and was built in 1953, twenty years after the Streamline Moderne design was popularised.

Rumblings are underway to make way for a larger pool for lane swimming as the oval shape is not favoured by users. The grand entrance apparently will be saved, let's hope so!

Boundary County Courthouse
Kootenai St, Bonners Ferry ID 83805
1941 Martin Fletcher

This courthouse building replaced a wooden building and cost $100,000 when it was built in 1941.

It has impressive decorative bas-relief panels depicting Idaho's main economy of the lumber industries, agriculture and mining.

Cassia County Courthouse
1459 Overland Ave, Burley ID 83318
1939 C.W. Watkins

The increase in commissioning official public buildings (WPA) during the interwar period left the mark of Art Deco firmly ingrained in many states including Idaho.

This symmetrical set-back and staggered building is constructed of red brick work and spandrels topped with square reliefs.

Idaho Falls Idaho Temple
1000 Memorial Dr, Idaho Falls ID 83402
1937-39 Architects - Edward O. Anderson, Ramm Hansen, John Fetzer, Lorenzo Snow Young, Hyrum Pope and Georgius Y. Cannon

This site was consecrated for this Church of the Latter-Day Saints in 1937 and in 1939 the Church leaders' broke ground. It was not completed until 1945 due to WWII. The exterior is reinforced concrete with a mixture of white quartz aggregate and white cement called cast stone.

John Regan American Legion Hall
401 W. Idaho St, Boise, ID 83702
1939 Tourtellotte & Hummel

This Legion Hall was designed and built by
the prolific architects *Tourtellotte &
Hummel*. It is described as being a hybrid
of Art Deco and modernist architecture.

Nuart Theatre
195 N Broadway St, Blackfoot ID 83221
1930 Walter DeMordaunt

This theatre and cinema were commissioned
and operated by *Paul Demordaunt* a local
entrepreneur who also administered the
Idaho theatre. It is now owned by Blackfoot
Community Players and has been listed on
the National Register of Historic Places since
1978.

Orpheum Theatre
146 Main Ave W, Twin Falls ID 83301
1921 J. H. Dodd

This theatre originally accommodated
900 people and it was in 1940 that it was
redesigned by the architect *Slack W.*

Winburn. Over
the years it has
served as a cinema and theatre and had several
owners. Since 2014 the current owners Larry and
Stephanie Johnso, and the Ovation Performing Arts
company have had ongoing restoration programmes in
place. It has an eclectic mix of events throughout the year,
including classic movies.

Romance Theatre
2 E Main St, Rexburg ID 83440
1916-17

The Romance theatre has had an exceedingly colourful history. It apparently opened in 1913, however, tragically the act of the Mona the Bullet Proof Women shockingly went wrong and she was fatally shot on the stage. It is likely that the theatre wanted to distance itself from this and re-emerged a few years later opening its doors again in 1917 for vaudeville and silent movies.

In 1976, the whole area was part of the Teton Dam disaster and much of the integral part of the theatre was destroyed, however, structurally it was still standing. The City of Rexburg acquired the theatre in 2005 and have since restored it back to its original condition.

Cloverleaf Creamery
205 Broadway Ave South, Buhl, ID 83316
c.1940s

This Streamline Moderne building was originally Smith's Dairy Products. After a renovation and it now serves a delicious selection of ice creams and related local products.

Star Theatre
322 State St, Weiser ID 83672
c.1917 Frank W. Moore

Originally a vaudevillian theatre named the Wheaton, the building then adapted for the silent movies of the day. In 1939 it underwent a restoration in the Art Deco style with its elaborate marquee.

It was added to the national register of historic places in 1999, and since 2001 the theatre has been owned and run by the Onion Skin Players, who are restoring it back to its original glory days.

Washington County Courthouse
256 E Court St, Weiser, ID 83672
1938-39 Tourtellotte & Hummel

This historic Government building was designed by the coveted architectural firm *Tourtellotte & Hummel* who were responsible for many of the Streamline Moderne/ Art Deco buildings in the state of Idaho.

Egyptian Theatre
700W Main Street, Boise ID 83702
1927 F. C. Hummel

This magnificent theatre and concert venue have been renovated and continues to be the oldest theatre operating in the City. Its elaborate features include the frescoes and Egyptian emblems adorning the interior and the great lotus pillars either side of the screen. These are authentically replicated from the pillars at Karnak.

ILLINOIS

Capital: Springfield
Became the 21st State: 1818
Flower: Violet
Bird: Cardinal

244   PALMOLIVE BUILDING, BY NIGHT, CHICAGO

ACCOMMODATION

Chicago Motor Club Hampton Inn
68 E Wacker Pl, Chicago, IL 60601
1928-29 Holabird & Root

This 17-story hotel is the former Headquarters of the Chicago Motor Club. The exterior is built of Bedford stone with a steel structure. It has an impressive large foyer with original plasterwork and a large hand painted map adorns one wall. The 143 guest rooms are in the modern contemporary style.

St Jane Hotel
230 N Michigan Ave, Chicago, IL 60601
1929 Burnham Bros.

This magnificent building is an icon of Chicago with its tower that resembles a champagne bottle. It has 364 guest rooms and luxurious suites. Formerly the Headquarters and offices of the Union Carbide and Carbon Company it has been transformed into a first-class hotel. The building has many original features including the elevators with ornate brass fittings. It has a sumptuous restaurant and cafe. The guest rooms in the tower have spectacular views of the city.

Kimpton Hotel Allegro
171 W Randolph St, Chicago, IL 60601

This hotel is the height of Art Deco glamour and luxury. All of the fittings and furnishings are in the style of the period. It has an Italian restaurant and a chic bar. The 483 guest rooms and suites are first class.

Intercontinental Hotel
505 Michigan Ave, Chicago, IL 60611
1929

This hotel has a long history of owners and renovations over the decades; however, it will always be synonymous with the roaring 20's. It was home to secret speakeasies; although, it was originally built as the exclusive Medinah Athletic Club. The construction was a display of wealth and opulence with a large bronze doorway, marble columns and a grand staircase. The cast bronze friezes and painted ceilings spared no expense and this hotel was known for its eminent guests. It has

undergone expansion and a 13 million renovation programme in 2015. It has 792 guest rooms and suites. An impressive swimming pool and restaurants and bars.

Palmer House Hilton Hotel
17 East Monroe St, Chicago, IL
1923-25 Holabird & Roche

This is the third hotel to stand on this site. The first was burnt down in the Great Chicago Fire of 1871, just 13 days after it opened to paying guests. The second hotel was raised to the ground to build a bigger and better designed building for the modern world. It has 1,639 guest rooms and suits making it the second largest hotel in the city. The interior is glamour and fitting of the opulent Art Deco era.

OUT & ABOUT

Pittsfield Cafe
55 E Washington St, Chicago, IL 60602

Hidden away in a grand
building you will find this
little authentic eatery. It's
well worth a little detour
to seek out.

Ceres Cafe
141 W Jackson Blvd, Chicago, IL 60604

This wonderful gem is set inside the Chicago Board of Trade building. The
interior is in keeping with the glorious Art Deco surroundings. It serves
great food and cocktails throughout the day and evening.

Nederlander/Oriental Theatre
24 W Randolph St, Chicago, IL 60601
1926 George L. & Cornelius W. Rapp

The James M. Nederlander Theatre was
originally the Oriental Theatre and the name is
synonymous with its sumptuous interior. It was
one of the first motion picture palaces with
decor inspired by the Far East.

It was in 2019 that it was renamed in honour of
Nederlander the legendary Broadway theatre
owner and producer. Be prepared to be dazzled by the highly decorative
luxurious interior.

Adler Planetarium
1300 S. Lake Shore Dr, Chicago, IL 60605
1930 Earnest A. Grunsfeld Jr.

This building is as popular today as it was
90 years ago. The colourful exterior walls
are constructed of pink granite and the
pleasing clean lines, sleekness and rotunda
bode well for the exhibitions on display.

Civic Opera Building
20 North Wacker Drive, Chicago, IL 60606
1929 Alfred Shaw

This gargantuan building is a fusion of styles blending Classical with Art Deco and International Style. It comprises of two 22 story wings and a central 44 story tower. It houses both the civic opera and the civic theatre in one of the wings.

Reebie Storage Warehouse
2325, 33 North Clark St, Chicago, IL 60614
1922 George S. Kingsley

This Egyptian Revival building is based on designs at the Temples of Dendera and Edfu. The owners who commissioned the building, brothers William and John Reebie wanted to create an authentic reproduction of ancient Egypt in their building. It was Fritz Albert who modelled the terracotta designs and he meticulously cross referenced his work with the originals held at the Art Institute and Field Museum.

Chicago Board of Trade Building
141 West Jackson Boulevard, Chicago, IL 60604
1930 Holabird & Root

This has to be one of the most impressive buildings in the whole of Chicago and an afternoon or morning can easily be spent enjoying its historical content. The building represents Hubris from Ancient Greek origin, constantly reminding traders of arrogance, overconfidence and foolish pride. The location of the building has an

immense presence, as it dominates the view on LaSalle Street appearing to block in the surrounding buildings. The building is adorned with relief sculptures and the large clock face is flanked by figures heads by sculptor *Alvin Meyer* and atop the building is the Goddess Ceres by *John Storr.* The marble columned interior is luxurious and this is where you will find the Ceres Café.

The Powhatan Building
4950 South Chicago Beach Drive
1929 R.S. De Golyer & Charles L. Morgan

This 22-story reinforced concrete building has a limestone facing with decorative colourful panel adorning the façade. The interior is equally as impressive, the foyer is a feast of Art Deco features and a basement swimming pool carries on the theme of American Indian influences.

The building is an exclusive luxury apartment block with only two condos on each floor making it exceptionally spacious. It is well worth a visit to view the exterior and during Open House weekend it is sometimes listed for public tours.

The Ritz Garage
5500 South Lake Park Ave, Chicago, IL 60637
1929 M. Louis Krogan

This 3-story ramp-style garage was designed to accommodate 400 vehicles. It has elaborate bas-reliefs depicting automobilia adorning the façade, including a playful roadster, signals, wheels and crankshaft. The garage has an impressive display of vintage vehicles to view.

MINNESOTA

Capital: St. Paul
Became the 32nd State: 1858
Flower: Ladyslipper
Sport: Ice Hockey

ACCOMMODATION

The Foshay
821 S Marquette Ave, Minneapolis, MN 55402
1929 Leon Eugene Arnal Magney & Tusler Inc.

This building a Marriott hotel was originally the home of W.B. Foshay Utility Company. In 2008 the building opened as the Foshay hotel after costing 90 million dollars to convert the 32-storey office tower. It is located downtown Minneapolis and has 229 guest rooms and suites.

It has an impressive 30th floor observation deck with 360-degree views of the historic area. It seamlessly blends Art Deco decadence with modern urban chic. Particularly nice is the Prohibition Sky bar on the 27fl that is the former boardroom of Wilbur Foshay.

The Westin Minneapolis
88 South 6th St, Minneapolis, MN 55402
1941-42 McEnary & Krafft

This landmark hotel is owned by Marriott and is set in the former Farmers & Mechanics Bank building. It displays a bas-relief either side of the entrance depicting a farmer and a mechanic designed by *Warren T. Mosman*. The hotel has 214 individual guest rooms and suites as they are all different shapes and sizes, due to the original layout of the bank. The main banking lobby has an impressive 30ft high ceiling and marble staircase with the original carved wooden emblems depicting the leading industries of World War II.

OUT & ABOUT

In the Heart of the Beast
1500 Lake St E, Minneapolis, MN 55407
1924 Ekman, Holm & Co.

Previously called the Avalon Theatre this splendid building is now a venue for puppet and mask theatre productions. It is supported by the Minnesota State Arts Board and offers an eclectic mix of performances throughout the year. Many of these are educational and free to the public.

Wells Fargo Center
90 South 7th St, Minneapolis, Minnesota 55402
1988 Cesar Pelli

You could easily believe that this building was constructed in the 1930s, however, you would be wrong. It was opened in 1988 and is the third tallest building in Minneapolis with 56 floors. It is aesthetically pleasing with the symmetry and setbacks on such a grand scale.

CenturyLink Building
200 S 5th Street, Minneapolis, Minnesota, 55402
1932 Hewitt & Brown

This 26-floor banking building was the second tallest in Minneapolis at 346ft. second only to the Foshay Tower, and in 1958 when it was extended to 416ft. The mass of the structure and its rising setbacks dominate the surrounding skyline. It is topped with an unusual microwave antenna. The beautiful limestone exterior changes colour during the day and evening.

Christ Church Lutheran
3244 34th Avenue S, Minneapolis 55406
1948 Eliel & Eero Saarinen

This church was designed by the *Saarinens'* the prolific and eminent Finnish-American father and son partnership. They were forward looking architects and this building is a forerunner for the next two decades. It is a listed historic monument and in 2011 the bell tower was renovated.

Fhima's Minneapolis
40 S. Seventh St, Minneapolis, MN 55402

This opulent restaurant is owned by restaurateur David Fhima since 2018, the menu is French and American orientated. The building has retained its original 1930s interior and prior to 2018 it was owned by Forum Cafeteria for 40 years.

Minneapolis Armory
500 South 6th St, Minneapolis, MN 55415
1936 P.C. Bettenburg & Walter H. Wheeler

This building has been utilised as an event venue since the late 1930s. The Hennepin County bought the armoury in 1989, with plans to place a new county jail on the site. This never came to fruition and the building is once again an event location that can house 8,400 people. It still has two hidden murals inside the building by *Elsa Jemne* and *Lucia Wiley* in the Social Realist style. This building was added to the NRHP in 1985.

Minneapolis Post Office
100 South 1st St, Minneapolis, MN 55401
1933 Leon Eugene Arnal

This mammoth building is constructed from granite and stone. It is 540 ft long and cost 4.5 million to build in 1933. It can also claim the prize for having the longest light fixture in the world at 350 ft weighing a colossal 16 tons and runs the entire length of the lobby. This light fixture was originally designed to assist in regulating the temperature of the building. Some of the bonus facilities for the employees were recreation rooms, a hospital unit as well as a rifle range that was housed in the basement.

Orpheum Theatre
910 Hennepin Ave, Minneapolis, MN 55403
1921 Roger Kirchoff et al.

In 1988 this theatre was sold by Bob Dylan (who owned it from 1979-1988) to the city of Minneapolis. It was renovated and reopened in 1993. It was originally named the Hennepin theatre.

The interior is impressive with a lobby that has six terracotta bas-relief sculptures and a domed ceiling containing 30,000 squares of aluminium leaf. The theatre seats 2,579 guests. The building was added to the NRHP in 1996.

Rand Tower
527 South Marquette Ave, Minneapolis, MN 55402
Holabird & Root 1929

This iconic tower was built for Rufus R. Rand who was a WWI aviator and was part of the family that owned the Minnesota Gas Company. In 1994 the building was added to the NRHP list.

It has the impressive sculpture called Wings in the lobby by *Oskar J.W. Hansen* who is best known for his sculptures at the Hoover Dam. The building is in the process of being converted into a 277-guest room hotel due to be opened at the end of 2020.

Washburn Park Water Tower
401 Prospect Ave, Minneapolis, MN 55419
1931 Harry Wild Jones

This water tower is situated on one of the highest points in South Minneapolis. It is 110 ft high and has the capacity to hold 1,350.000 gallons of water. It has eight guardians of health that encircle the tower to ward off evil spirits and eight eagles by *John Karl Daniels* that are located at the top of the structure to keep a beady eye out.

Uptown Theatre
2906 Hennepin Ave, Minneapolis, MN 55408
1939 Liebenburg & Caplan

This Streamline Moderne theatre was rebuilt in 1939 following a fire. It has two incised roundels on the exterior stone facade that portray themes of adventure and travel in the cinema. It has one screen with a seating capacity of 350.

The Commodore Bar & Restaurant
79 Western Ave N, St Paul, MN 55102
1920

Recently restored to its full glory this famous establishment is the only remaining original Jazz age bar and restaurant in St Pauls. It has elegance and decadence in equal measures. It originally opened as a hotel and during the prohibition years a basement speakeasy served amongst others the legendary *F. Scott Fitzgerald.*

Mickey's Diner
36 West 7th St, St Paul, MN 55102
1937

In 1937 this prefabricated
building was constructed by
Jerry O'Mahony Diner Co.
of Elizabeth New Jersey and
was shipped to St Paul by
rail. It has been on the
historic register since 1983.
It is 50ft by 10ft with red
and yellow porcelain-
enamelled steel panels and
a row of ten train style
windows to the front of the
diner.

Canby Theatre
109 St Olaf Ave N, Canby, MN 56220
1939 Perry E. Crosier

Originally this grand theatre seated
600 and it was in 2015 that it was
totally renovated. It now has the
capacity to seat 210 in screen one and
75 people in screen two.

Cozy Theater
223 Jefferson St S, Wadena, MN 56482
1938 Kirby Snyder

This cinema was originally built in 1914 and it
was later remodelled in 1938 incorporating its
streamline marquee and Art Deco features. It
has three screens with a seating capacity of 600.

NEW YORK

Capital: Albany
Became the 11th State: 1788
Fruit: Apple
Bird: Bluebird

ACCOMMODATION

Hotel Edison
228 West 47th Street, NY 10036
1931 Herbert J Krapp

It was Thomas Alva Edison who was honoured with opening this hotel by turning on the lights and it's named after the American inventor. It attracted the hoi-polloi of the day and has an impressive high-ceilinged   Art Deco entrance and foyer.

The 810 guest rooms are in a pared down modernist style. An adjoining restaurant and bar serve throughout the day and it is very conveniently located for Time Square being a 3-minute walk away.

JW Marriott Essex House New York
160 Central Park South, NY 10019
1931 Frank Grad & Sons

This 44-story hotel, with its suitably inspired deco interior has 426 guest rooms, and a further 101 suites that overlook Central Park. The two restaurants, spa and fitness centre, make this a very inviting place to stay. However, it is the large iconic red neon rooftop sign announcing Essex House, that greets you from afar.

The New Yorker Hotel
481 8th Avenue, NY 10001
1930 Sugarman & Berger

The New Yorker a Wyndham hotel, opened on the 2nd of January 1930, and originally had 2,503 guest rooms starting at $3.50 per night.

After a full restoration programme, it has 1050 guest rooms and suites. The luxurious foyer and decadent interior have a coffee shop and restaurant, operating 24 hours. Adorning the facade of the hotel is the iconic red block New Yorker lettering.

Carlyle Hotel
35 East 76ᵗʰ Street, NY 10021
1930 Bien & Prince

This elegant and exclusive luxury hotel has 190 guest rooms and suites with views of Central Park. The opulent interior is a fusion of styles, The Gallery restaurant is inspired by the sultan's dining room at the Topkapi Palace in Turkey. The Cafe Carlyle celebrates the golden age of New York cabaret with

regular top names in jazz and the entertainment business performing. However, it is the Bemelmans Bar (named after the author of the classic Madeline children books) that showcases its Art Deco interior with the 24-carat gold leaf covered ceiling, metal-trimmed black glass top tables and large murals. Once visited, always remembered, this hotel has something for everyone.

Waldorf Astoria
301 Park Avenue, NY 10022
1929-31 Schultze & Weaver

This Waldorf Astoria originally opened in 1893 commissioned by millionaire William Waldorf Astor, it moved to its present location in 1931 from one a little further south on Fifth Avenue, and it still retains some of the original Art Deco interior. The lobby has the decadent feel of a ballroom with its sweeping marble staircases.

The hotel has recently undergone an extensive multimillion-dollar refurbishment and fortunately the famous exterior has been preserved and protected. The renovations and refurbishment have seen a fresher new style being adopted in the hotel; this has not detracted from the Art Deco aesthetics. It has 1,300 guest rooms and suites and has first class restaurants and bars.

Plaza Hotel
768 5ᵗʰ Avenue, NY 10019
1907 Henry J. Hardenberg

This famous hotel is synonymous with the jazz age and its writers in particular F. Scott Fitzgerald and his wife Zelda. Located on the 18th floor of the hotel, is the 900sq ft suite that includes Art Deco features and pieces of period furniture, with photos of the author and his wife. More unexpected additions to the décor include gramophone-shaped iphone-compatible speakers and vitrines that will house sporting trophies supposedly won by Tom Buchanan, a prominent character in the film. Fans of the Great Gatsby book will know that part of the novel takes place here. F. Scott Fitzgerald even danced in its fountain with his wife Zelda. The 300 guest rooms and suites are decorated in the beaux arts style, unless you choose the extravagant penthouse Art Deco suites. The champagne bar and restaurant will not disappoint.

The Chatwal
130 West 44ᵗʰ Street, NY 10036
1905 Stanford White

This fabulously opulent and decadent hotel has 76 exquisite guest rooms and suites. The Art Deco experience starts in the foyer and continues all the way to the famous Art Deco style *Lambs Club*, restaurant and bar. The guest rooms are high tech so be prepared for those extra special comforts.

Sherry-Netherland Hotel
781 5th Ave, NY 10022
1927 Schultze & Weaver

This exclusive boutique hotel has 50 guest rooms and suites overlooking Central Park. It houses the

 famous Harry Cipriani restaurant which is a duplicate of the famed Harry's bar in Venice. With the added extras of a 'his and hers' hairdressing salon this luxurious hotel ticks all the boxes.

The Surrey
20 East 76th St, NY 10021
1926

This stylish hotel has 189 guest rooms and suites decorated in a modern warm contemporary style. It has Art Deco touches throughout with the light fittings and elements of the decor. The Cafe Boulud restaurant and bar are reminiscent of a bygone era, and sipping a cocktail here is a special experience.

Radio City Apartments
142 West 49th Street, NY 10019

These affordable apartments are located a block away from Radio City Music Hall. The

112 guest rooms and suites have varying

facilities, some are equipped with kitchenettes others have two bedrooms. The large penthouse suite has fine views over the city.

Bryant Hotel
40 West 40th Street, New York, NY
1924 Raymond Hood

This building started life as the American Standard Radiator Building and the architectural splendour created by *Raymond Hood* incorporated black brick with gold setbacks and terracotta. Despite this being a relatively small building in comparison to others in the city of the period, the design gives the impression of a denser larger exterior. By utilising long slim windows and dark brickwork it emphasises the bulk of the building.

It was transformed into a luxury hotel in 2001 and has won many awards for its design. The 128 guest rooms and suites are ultra-modern in design and the Japanese Koi restaurant, along with the newly established Celon Cocktail Bar and Lounge are superb.

Roosevelt Hotel
45 E 45th St, NY 10017
1924 George B. Post

This jazz age hotel has a colourful history of hosting the rich and famous from around the World. One of its claims to fame is the first broadcast of 'Auld Lang Syne' sang by Guy Lombardo and his orchestra in 1929 becoming the traditional New

Year's Eve anthem. Lombardo and his orchestra were resident at the Roosevelt Grill for the next 30 years. It has also been the backdrop to many films, shows over the decades. There are 1,025 guest rooms and suites in this glamourous and highly sought-after hotel that is located near to Central Station.

Affinia Hotel
371 7ᵗʰ Avenue at 31ˢᵗ Street, NY 10001

Designed by the acclaimed Rockwell Group, the Manhattan NYC's 618 guest rooms and suites bring a refreshing downtown look to midtown. Striking a balance between residential and stylish, select suites are over

1,000 square feet — larger than most New York City apartments — and come complete with kitchens. Up-to-the-minute amenities are provided, including 37-inch flat screen TVs, workspace with oversized desks, and high-speed Internet access.

WestHouse Hotel
201 West 55ᵗʰ Street, NY 10019

This hotel seamlessly merges modern with Art Deco and exudes opulence luxury and style. It has 172 guest rooms and suites with a rooftop restaurant and glamorous bar.

OUT & ABOUT

Radio City Music Hall
1260 6th Ave, New York, NY 10020
1932 Edward Durrell Stone & Donald Deskey

Synonymous with New York is Radio City Music Hall, and it has to be on the top of your Art Deco list of places to visit. It covers the expanse of 2 acres and has the capacity to seat 5,960 visitors. It is all part of the larger complex of the Rockefeller Center (established by the American Rockefeller family, who were the wealthiest businessmen of their time) and was fully restored and renovated in 1999.

It hosts concerts, stage shows and the legendary Christmas Spectacular. The exterior of the building has a large wraparound marquee with neon signage and above the entrance are six bronze plaques of musicians playing instruments by Hildreth Meiere (1892-1961). The opulent auditorium is on a series of levels and the lavish interior is designed by Donald Deskey (1894-1989).

Throughout the year the biggest names in showbiz appear here, however, it is the World-famous yearly Christmas Spectacular that is such a crowd pleaser.

Rockefeller Center
45 Rockefeller Plaza, New York, NY 10111

The Rockefeller Center is the dreamchild of John D. Rockefeller Jr to create a cultural center for New Yorkers and the world to admire. It comprises of buildings, shops, restaurants, a skating rink, and gardens. He employed the best sculptures and designers to create magnificent monuments to the arts. These pay homage to man's development in industry, science and spirit harnessing the elements. Lee Lawrie (1877-1963) one of the

most significant sculptors of the time designed the most dazzling entrance piece in his depiction of 'Wisdom'. This gargantuan artwork looks out over the ice rink (in winter) and whether you view it up close or from a distance it is mesmerising.

You can easily spend a couple of hours sitting on a bench conveniently placed nearby and gaze upwards to this heavenly and spiritual masterpiece. This being said the other highly impressive bas-reliefs that are to be found on the Rockefeller buildings are also perfection. It is well worth taking the official guided tour to get the full history, these can be purchased online or in the center. The walking tour guide lasts about an hour and all the main features are pointed out. Another popular excursion is the 'Top of the Rock' experience. Just like visiting the top of

the Empire State Building ascending the heights of the Rockefeller Building affords rewarding views. Beat the que. tickets are available, however, if you arrive first thing in the morning, the waiting time is minimal.

Of course, it is always better to choose a bright cloudless day, this is not always possible so I recommend a trip up the Rock or the Empire State Building in the late evening as seeing the City in all its neon glory is well worth the hike.

The relief of Wisdom depicted here just out of view is Light and Sound located at, 30 Rockefeller Centre.

Pictured left is the Polychromatic bas-relief also by Lawrie Lee titled - The Genius Who Interprets to the Human Race the Laws and Cycles of the Cosmic Figures of the Universe, Making the Cycles of Sight and Sound. Located at 25 West 50th St, Rockefeller Centre.

Left is the sculpture of Prometheus (Paul Manship 1885-1966) resides over the annual ice rink that is situated in front of the main entrance to the Rockefeller Building.

Right is the 45ft bronze Statue of Atlas also by Lee Lawrie in 1937, stands resplendently within the main courtyard of the Rockefeller Center. The combination of buildings and art work that 'make up' the Rockefeller dynasty's legacy are astonishing.

Gold Winged God of Mercury - Lee Lawrie

Chrysler Building

405 Lexington Ave, New York, NY 10174
1930 William Van Alen

The Chrysler Building is probably one of the most photographed and liked buildings in New York and has 77 floors. This skyscraper is all that Art Deco encompasses; its lavish, glamourous and exudes opulence and success. It was built as the headquarters of the Chrysler motor company and no expense was spared in creating a building fit for purpose. That purpose being to showcase the company in a fashionable and modern style while advertising outwardly the capabilities of this particular motor industry.

Take time to focus on the elements of the building, the eagle car mascots, the car tyre details and nuts and bolts. This whole building in its glimmering steel is representing the Chrysler car, it is the biggest billboard manufactured!

Not content with the exterior, the main foyer is a feast of terrazzo and marble facia. It has marquetry maps and polished brass. From floor to ceiling the elaborate and ornate design is to impress and it certainly does this. Please note that it is free to enter the lobby and take photographs, but strictly no phone videos are allowed.

Grand Central Station
89 E 42nd St, New York, NY 10017

This World-famous Beaux Arts landmark building predates Art Deco and Modernism, in its design, however, the building is closely associated with that period. Post the depression era it prospered and the Grand Central Terminal was not only a transport hub it housed an art gallery, an art school and a news reel movie theatre. The following decades saw its decline and fall and it was not until the 1990s that this historically important building was fully renovated; after facing serious dereliction and possible demolition. It now houses over 60 shops and 35 places to eat. It covers 48 acres and has an amazing 44 platforms to countrywide destinations.

Empire State Building
20 W 34th St, New York, NY 10001
1931 Shreve, Lamb & Harmon

This Art Deco skyscraper is a 102-story high office building that has an observation deck for the general public at its summit. It stood as the World's tallest building for 40 years until 1970. The design has various setbacks and a large antenna making it over 1,450ft tall.

It is open daily for visits to its viewing deck and if you arrive early it is not needed to buy the more expensive 'beat the queue tickets', the grand foyer is marble clad with terrazzo flooring and the metal work on the elevators is unmissable. It is well worth visiting during the daytime and evening to experience the best of both.

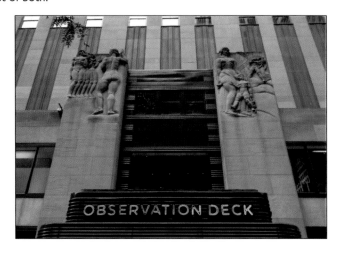

Chez Josephine Restaurant
414 W 42nd St, NY 10036

The Chez Josephine French restaurant is an homage to the great lady herself. It was established by one of Josephine Baker's children in 1986 and is a favourite spot for pre-theatre

dinners. The interior is lavish and certainly sets the scene for a night out in NYC with the nightly live piano entertainment. Be prepared to book in advance as it gets very busy.

The Monkey Bar
60 E 54th St, New York, NY 10022

This atmospheric restaurant is located within Hotel Elysee was established in 1936. It started life as a dimly lit depression era venue that lived off its reputation for risqué songs and was frequented by the bohemian set of the day. The colourful hand painted murals are by Charlie Wala

and were completed in the 1950s and it is a vision of opulence and glamourous. It has been used in filmsets and seen in Sex in the City and Mad Men.

Chanin Building
122 East 42nd St, NY
1928 Irwin Channin

This impressive 56 story building was originally designed as leasable office space and it still serves this purpose today. The architect also responsible for other notable buildings in New York chose the building for his own offices on the top floor.

The exterior of the building is buff brick limestone with a terracotta tower. It has a series of setbacks and a crenelated crown. It has a bronze frieze located at the street level depicting the sea creatures of amoeboid that turn into jellyfish that in turn into fish that change into geese.

This was the story of evolution being told as the building was designed to be educational and fun. The interior of the building is also impressive with its opulent decor and lighting.

Metropolitan Life Insurance Company
200 Park Ave, New York, NY 10017
1929 Harvey Wiley Corbett & D. Everett Waid

This building needed to expand and in 1929 the North Building was designed and the 29-story addition was constructed in four pieces that took 17 years to complete. An ornate walkway connects 11 Madison with the rest of the MetLife building.

1 Wall Street
New York, NY 1005
1931 Ralph Walker

Originally this was the Irving Trust Company and the 50-story building is as beautiful on the inside as the out. It features setbacks and a decorative

faceted façade. The reception room is
designed by Hildreth Meier and is known
as the Red Room with its red, orange and
gold mosaic tiles that were made in Berlin.

If this was not enough to dazzle the
visitors that visited the Banking hall then
the observation room on the 49th floor was sure too, as it has high vaulted ceilings
adorned with mother of pearl sea shells from the Philippines. The building has been
repurposed and renovated opening the beginning of 2020, with its 566 highly prized
condominiums, and the Red Room is now part of the lower floors shopping
emporium, for all to enjoy.

.

29 Broadway
New York, NY 10006
1931 Sloan & Robertson

This shopping mall and condominium building has many
Art Deco features including the geometric pattern on
the white marble façade.   Like many Art Deco
buildings, it is the lobby that showcases features of the
exuberant and showstopping glamour of the age. The
aluminium leaf ceiling and sculpted Cippolino marble,
along with the handrails and lighting fittings are superb.

25 Central Park West
New York, NY 10023
1931 Irwin Chanin

This apartment block known as 'The Century; has two towers of topped by complex crowns, featuring vertical fluting and cantilevered floor plates. The interior lobby has impressive curvilinear details. It was converted into condominiums in 1987 and has a total of 410 apartments over 32 floors.

1001 Jerome Ave
Bronx, New York, NY 10452
1929 Horace Ginsberg & Associates

This is one of the Bronx's first Art Deco apartment buildings and is located near to the Yankees Stadium. It is 11 story high and the main focal point is the polychromatic terracotta decoration on the exterior.

Fish Building
Grand Concourse, Bronx, New York, NY
? Horace Ginsberg & Associates

This building derives its name from the brightly coloured sea life mosaic that adorns its façade. Other notable features are the steel canopy with a decorative fluted edge and the inside of the lobby can boast of two murals by Rene and CP Graves.

The elevator doors are wonderfully decorative and these are complemented by the stained-glass windows and terrazzo floor.

888 Grand Concourse
Bronx, New York, NY 10451
1937 Emery Roth

This apartment building is particularly of interest with its use of materials to highlight its features in steel, black granite, bronze along with marble mosaic and gold stripping.

Bronxdale Swimming Pool
2016 Bronxdale Avenue, Bronx, New York, NY 10462
1928

Alas, this is no longer a swimming pool, however, the glorious façade is still available to enjoy as the Bronx Park Medical Pavilion. It is a simplistic and effective form of horizontal and vertical lines.

Rego Park Jewish Center
9730 Queens Blvd, Flushing, New York, NY 11374
1948 Frank Grad & Sons

This Streamline Moderne architectural style building with its simplistic façade has an impressive mural by A. Raymond Katz the Hungarian born artist. The interior has Art Deco features and stained-glass windows.

Mccarrren Park Pool & Play Center
McCarren Park, Brooklyn, New York, NY 11222

This WPA (Works Progress Administration) building is Streamline Moderne, it reopened in 2012 after a multi-million-dollar renovation programme and is now the Aymar Embury II complex.

711 Brightwater Court
Brooklyn, New York, NY 11235
1934 Martyn N. Weinstein

This building is located in Brighton Beach and is a masterwork of ornamentation on its façade. It has zig-zag brickwork, and colourful glazed terracotta tile work. The feature of black and gold decoration around the front door is an added bonus on this first-rate building.

Ambassador Apartments
30 Daniel Low Terrace, Staten Island,
New York, NY 10301
1932 Lucian Pisciatta

This apartment block has the most elaborate terracotta entrance that can be seen repeated to a lesser extent over the rest of the building. The coloured tiles feature Art Deco designs and the brick façade has spandrels displaying different geometric designs including the frozen waterfall theme. The lobby is parred down being modernist in style. Famous names such as Paul Newman and Martin Sheen are previous occupiers.

Lane Theatre
168 New Dorp Lane, New York, NY
1938 John Eberson

This modernist style theatre is a rare survivor by the prolific cinema architect *Eberson*. It was commissioned by the Moses brothers who were the top entrepreneurial theatre owners of the time. Despite its size the entrance is dominated by a large marquee and oversize signage. The interior is just as impressive and it fortunately survived intact, apart from the the abstract murals.

Paramount Theatre
560 Bay Street, Stapleton, Staten Island, New York, NY 10304
1930 Rapp & Rapp

The exterior of this theatre gives the impression of the grandeur of a skyscraper with its large ziggurat façade. This is, however, deceptive as the colourful red brick frontage was constructed for show. The building is in fact very small and designed with clean lines and machine age precision. It unfortunately has had several attempts at renovation, unfortunately the costs made it not viable for the owners. Its future is still hangs in the balance.

WYOMING

Capital: Cheyenne
Became the 44th State: 1890
Gemstone: Jade
Sport: Rodeo

1154—Main Street, Sheridan, Wyo.

ACCOMMODATION

The Historic Plains Hotel
1600 Central Ave, Cheyenne, WY 82001
1911

This hotel was established by a lady named Astrid whose father was a diplomat and travelled the World. As a child she would accompany her father on his overseas trips being exposed to fine art and culture. When she grew-up her natural entrepreneurial flair was ploughed into property development and she established this hotel, with its 131 guestrooms and suites.

It has a quality restaurant and the Wigwam bar, with the added bonus of being close to the museums and galleries.

During the 1920s and 1930s, it would host the dignitaries and celebrities of the day and still has that aura of a grand presence. It is a fusion of styles and Art Deco has left its footprint. Be specific when booking to secure the green Art Deco bathroom.

OUT & ABOUT

Napoli's Restaurant
1901 Central Ave, Cheyenne, WY 82001
1937

This building was the former Frontier hotel. It now has apartments on the upper floors and Napoli's Italian restaurant on the ground floor. The original canopy and terracotta tiles still adorn the facade up to the first floor.

The Arts and Sciences Auditorium
University of Wyoming, Laramie, WY
1936 William DuBois

Formerly known as the Liberal Arts Building, on the University campus, this building was constructed with funding from the PWA (Public Works Administration) during the depression years, that lasted from 1929-1941. The University site has expanded over the decades; this building is still considered to be iconic of the Art Deco era.

Hyart Theater
251 E Main St, Lovell, WY 82431
1950 H.D. Bischoff

This theatre and cinema is still owned and run by the Bischoff family and it was added to the NRHP in 2009 and is known for its exceptional exterior. The building has a turquoise coloured metal lattice screen that covers a pink metal facade and a tall neon pylon sign. It seats 975 guests and true to its nature being a family cinema, no films over a 12 rating are screened.

Boeing/United Airline Terminal Building Hangar and Fountain
Cheyenne, WY
1929-1934 F. Porter Sr. of Austin Co.

The combination of the terminal, hangar and fountain were built between 1929-34. Cheyenne Municipal Airport was once a major transport facility. The fountain was commissioned as a memorial to early aviation history.

Wyoming State Museum
Barrett Building, 2301 Central Avenue, Cheyenne, WY 82002

Well worth a visit is this interesting well-equipped museum. Particularly nice are the vintage vehicles on display and comprehensive history of the early to mid-twentieth century. The mission of the museum is to serve as an educational, historical and cultural institution and it certainly lives up to this.

Art Deco as an architectural style and design is to be found in all States in the USA to a lesser or more degree. Below is the exuberant Auburn Cord Duesenberg Automobile Museum Store from 1930, located in Auburn, Indiana. Just one more of the thousands of Deco delights just waiting for you to discover.

These photos are courtesy of a fellow Art Deco enthusiast and friend, Lavon Kara Brown.

GLOSSARY

Arts & Crafts - This social and artistic movement was active the latter part of the 19th century. Among its main proponents were William Morris, John Ruskin and Walter Crane. Charles Rennie Macintosh, who was an exponent of the Glasgow School. It came about as a reaction to industrialisation and mass-produced goods. The idle was to produce bespoke handcrafted items for the masses, however this was not feasible due to the intensive hours of labour and production costs. This meant only the richer people could afford the items, which was in complete juxtaposition to the mandate of the movement.

Art Nouveau - This style of arts and design was popular c.1890-1910 and is recognisable with its references to nature and organic sinuous designs. Often these designs would include a female form with long flowing hair. The style transferred to jewellery, glass ware, illustration and architecture. Among the main proponents of the time were; Aubrey Beardsley, Louis Comfort Tiffany, Antoni Gaudi, Max Beckmann and Alphonse Mucha.

Curvilinear - Design in a building consisting of curved flowing lines, employed in Streamline Moderne buildings.

Functionalism - This architectural and design style made popular by the Bauhaus advocated that buildings should be designed based solely on the purpose and function of the building. It opposed unnecessary adornments and decoration to the building.

Marquee - A roof like structure, often bearing a signboard, projecting over an entrance, of a theatre or hotel.

Oculus - A circular window (porthole) which is a familiar feature in Art Deco buildings especially when a reference to the sea or ocean liners is predominant in the architecture.

Parallelepiped - This is a three-dimensional building, formed by six parallelograms.

Streamline Moderne - Emerged in the 1930s. Its architectural style emphasised curving forms, long horizontal lines and sometimes nautical elements. As seen in ocean liner designed buildings and some lidos. It resonated the times of technological advancement and is associated with the innovations of high-speed motors cars and aeroplanes.

Vernacular - An architectural style that is designed based on the local needs and the availability of construction materials, reflecting and incorporating local traditions.

WPA – Workers Progress Administration was founded in 1935 by the American New Deal Agency, employing millions of job seekers to carry out public works projects, assisting to alleviate the depression era.

Saving our Art Deco Heritage

Having travelled extensively over the years for business and pleasure, I have felt privileged and honoured to have; slept in, dined at, drank in, swam in, and laughed in, some of our most phenomenal twentieth century architecture. To have sat in the most exquisite Art Deco furniture and drank from striking tea cups; Art Deco touches every nuance of our lives. No architectural movement or style has had such an effect on so many people and objects before. It is unique and that is why we have to preserve, and restore our twentieth century heritage for future generations to enjoy.

I am always saddened to hear that a place I have visited has been demolished to make way for a new development or that is it was too expensive to upkeep a building or lido despite local outcry. However, I am euphoric when I hear that a *Peoples Trust* has been formed with a plan to raise the profile of a building and ultimately restore it back to its former glory.

I urge any person who has a passion for Art Deco to seek out your nearest monument and support it. It is no good just to save these iconic buildings, they then need to be patronised to keep them viable.

My hat goes off (and I have many) to all you dedicated and hardworking people who often go unrecognised, we all owe you our wholehearted gratitude for helping to save our iconic Art Deco heritage.

Lastly but certainly not least, thank you to all the Art Deco Societies' in the USA and around the World for championing, celebrating, highlighting and protecting our Art Deco Heritage.

Thank You!

Credits & Acknowledgements

Where to start....it has to be with my editor, Elizabeth, her endless hours of devoted time spent in making sense of my scribblings, writings and 2am messages! I wholeheartedly appreciate her expertise and input, Thank You. To all my family, friends and colleagues, who have supported me in all my ventures and rallied me on when needed.

My sincere thanks to the hotels, restaurants, cinemas, theatres and tourist boards who have kindly allowed me to use photographs and supplied me with additional information. To all the Art Deco Societies throughout the world who are not only my kindred spirits, they are helping to preserve, educate and entertain future generations, about our Art Deco heritage.

My thanks to Margaret Young the artist who captured my better side. And finally, but certainly not least, to Richard, whose encouragement and culinary skills have always kept me on track!

Any further information can be obtained at www.artdeco-traveller.co.uk

Index